PRAISE FOR *TURNING A*

"I found this book to be as practical as it is profound, as simple as it is insightful. Paula Hirschboeck is the consummate Zen teacher in her ability to use words to move beyond words. In the frightening midst of our threatened planet, she gently invites the reader to realize the sustaining inter-connecting energy of the Universe. We can turn because we are being turned."

—Paul Knitter
Paul Tillich Emeritus Professor of Theology and Religions,
Union Theological Seminary, NYC. Author of
—*One Earth Many Religions: Multifaith
Dialogue and Global Responsibility*
—*Without Buddha I Could Not Be Christian*

"In *Turning and Being Turned: A Zen Circle of Practice Realization*, Prajnatara Paula Hirschboeck invites the reader into conversation with the wisdom of Zen Master Dogen. Offering a clarifying perspective on some commonly misunderstood approaches to Zen, it is also a "how to" book, providing readers with creative exercises that will enliven their practice beyond the meditation cushion. Prajnatara's exploration will help readers expand their view beyond the personal turning to discover how we are all turned by the world in a dance of reciprocity."

—Renshin Barbara Verkuilen, M.S. Soto Zen Priest
Author of *Dokusan with Dogen: Timeless Lessons in
Negotiating the Way, The Tale of Zen Master Bho Li* and
co-author of *Tending the Fire: An Introspective
Guide to Zen Awakening.*

"This refreshing read serves as an excellent high-energy infusion of Zen Buddhist Dharma, clear enough to guide the uninitiated and simultaneously penetratingly refined for the experienced practitioner. Prajnatara Paula Hirschboeck accomplishes this task in a spirited way that addresses both our global commonality and our personal uniqueness as the text washes over us while leaving ample space to challenge the reader."

—Seiso Paul Cooper
Author of *The Zen Impulse and the Psychoanalytic Encounter;
Zen Insight, Psychoanalytic Action: Two Arrows Meeting*

"This handbook for Zen practice contains a medley of offerings. Among them are many quotes from Eihei Dogen and the author's teacher that can be used for meditative contemplation; glimpses of the author's spiritual journey from ministry as a Dominican sister to her current Zen teaching; and several essays by her students on how to use creative aspects—photography, drawing, poetry, mandala, soul collage, writing and dance—to help enliven a practice traditionally centered upon silent seated meditation."

—*Jan Chozen Bays, Co-Abbot of Heart of Wisdom Temple in Portland, OR and Great Vow Monastery.*
Author of many books on mindfulness and healing and also a pediatrician. Her latest book is *Mindful Medicine: 40 Simple Practices to Help Healthcare Professionals Heal Burnout and Reconnect to Purpose*

"To follow a spiritual path is to turn and be turned. I am grateful for this collection of practices (including gratitude practice!) and all the "turning words" that gently turn us towards a new way of understanding life on Earth and a new way of being part of it."

— David Loy
Author of *Ecodharma: Buddhist Teaching for the Ecological Crisis*

TURNING AND BEING TURNED

A Zen Circle of Practice Realization

TURNING AND BEING TURNED

A Zen Circle of Practice Realization

PRAJNATARA PAULA HIRSCHBOECK

Henschel
HAUS
publishing, inc.
Milwaukee, Wisconsin

Published by HenschelHAUS Publishing, Inc.
Milwaukee, Wisconsin
www.henschelHAUSbooks.com

ISBN: 978159598-895-9
E-ISBN: 978159598-896-6
LCCN: 2022932819

Printed in the United States of America.

TABLE OF CONTENTS

DEDICATION

At the heart of everything is relationship. This book is the creation of myriad relationships arising from our common source, the ineffable Universe.

I dedicate it to some specific magnificent beings who helped me bring it forth:

- my Zen teacher of thirty years, Sojun Diane Martin, Roshi

- the women of Sophia Zen Sangha, open and gracious teachers for me,

- my parents, Rosemary and John, my loving family and supportive friends,

- my partner, Susan, who always reminds me "animals are people too."

- And to the Honey Locust tree outside my window – kindly bent to ease me as this book took form; rooting me in the dream of the Earth.

FOREWORD

Prajnatara Paula Hirschboeck offers us *Turning and Being Turned: A Zen Circle of Practice Realization* as a handbook, and it fulfills this function in the richest of ways. It is an instruction manual and a road map to the ineffable. It is a guide to realms without definable dimensions. And it also takes the reader by the hand. It is the warmest, kindest of guides into these realms. This book of Zen teachings is unique in its capacity to explore complex concepts with such down-to-Earth assurance and generosity.

Turned and Being Turned includes the reader from the very first word. Prajnatara Paula lets us know she is with us. She asks questions and provides us with highlighter, eraser, and review points. She teaches us how to meet a turning phrase, moment, or feeling without evasion. She tells us to "notice what feelings, memories, or associations bubble up. Listen to the phrase through your body. Please resist asking "What does this mean?" This handbook is an owner's manual for the mind that encounters wisdom.

Anchored in the teachings of Eihei Dogen and Sojun Diane Martin Roshi, Prjanatara Paula includes her own discoveries as a student of the Dharma with those of her students in Sophia Zen Sangha. The book is centered on Dogen's circular and intereelated stages of practice as realization. Selections from his work are beautifully described and brought to life for the reader. Prajnatara Paula prompts us with questions to consider, techniques for deepening into the teachings, and concrete instructions for moving within Dogen's Circle. She doesn't just describe the vivid truth of interrelatedness; she gives it to us.

This book intersects current societal planetary crises with our daily choice to awaken. It's wide reach connects classic Buddhist teachings, Christian mystics, and fascinating quotes ranging from *Alice in Wonderland* to the deep ecology of Joanna Macy. Prajnatara Paula has an intuitive capacity for integrating ideas with practical choices. The handbook is well-attuned to bring the reader to new capacities.

The best of Buddhist writing brings the experience it describes; imprints the reader and not just the pages. This book opens us in just such a way, with kind reminders to be attentive, appreciative, intimate. Receive this book even as it teaches you to "receive the teachings of the seasons, of rocks and shorelines, of burning embers and misty rain, as they reveal themselves to you. They are dharma doors." The book's door is open wide; please walk in.

—Beth Jacobs, PhD
Lay transmitted Soto Zen Teacher
Author of *The Original Buddhist Psychology,*
A Buddhist Journal, and *Long Shadows of Practice*

ACKNOWLEDGMENTS

First, a deep bow of gratitude to my writing mentor, Pamela Johnson. In late March 2020, in the chilly, open air of her garage, Pamela offered to help me explore the possibility of writing a book. Her insightful questioning and deep listening led me to discover and refine my intention as it evolved. She helped me navigate the steep learning curve and complexities of publication. I'm blessed in Pamela, a writing expert who is also a soul sister.

Thank you to Dominican sister Marie Lucek, who somehow managed to transfer piles of handwritten pages into a typed document I could work with.

As revision upon revision came forth, many readers were generous with their time and thoughtful suggestions. Thank you to Renshin Barbara Verkuilen, Sheryl Lilke, Rob Fromberg, Clare Wagner, Mary Schneider, Beth Jacobs, Seiso Paul Cooper, Elizabeth Turner, David McKee, and Maeve Pharmer.

Finally, gratitude to Kira Henschel of HenschelHAUS Publishing. To this beginner in the unknown terrain of typesetting, proofs, marketing and more, Kira's expertise feels |miraculous. Her patience, flexibility, and personal support is ever encouraging.

... Night after night, the shining stars appear.

Is it not perhaps a convocation

of the compassionate?

—Crouching Dragon Abbess Yin Yue
(17th Century China)

—Daughters of Emptiness: Poems of Chinese Buddhist Nuns
by Beata Grant

CHAPTER ONE

An Opening

Introducing Ourselves

Thank you for opening these pages to study and practice with me. Simply choosing to do so is participation in the awakening of humanity's consciousness. Our moment is the opportunity for an energy shift called "The Great Turning." Human evolution is currently at a turning point for recreating our species. (1)

On October 26, 2021, just before the Climate Summit convened, I heard UN Secretary General Antonio Guterres challenge world leaders: "You can still make this a turning point into the future instead of a tipping point into climate catastrophe."

A turning point toward a viable future cannot be determined by world leaders. This handbook focuses on the small turnings of our personal choices toward wiser, kinder care for ourselves and humanity, so all living beings may share a vibrant Earth community. It is yours to use "hands on." This book keeps micro and macro views connected. As we negotiate the book's map of practice, we will "zoom in" to our unique situation and also "zoom out" to connect it with societal and global concerns. Collective energy for The Great Turning will only gain momentum from personal choices individual humans are making now. That's you. That's me.

Turning and Being Turned

This is a handbook of Zen Buddhist teachings. It offers many ways to turn into the practice of realizing we are being turned by a bigger, more mysterious reality than what is available to our small selves.

Take note when key terms are either capitalized or in lower case. For example, you will see *"small self"* and *"Big"* or *"True Self,"* the *personal*, relative view and the *Universal*, Absolute view, the changing physical *universe* and the eternal, spiritual *Universe*.

With practice, we discover that the perceptions of a small, separate self are faulty. We gradually realize the Wisdom that sees the personal and the Universal, micro and macro, as one reality. Your unique, physical reality—your life—is the way to realize an enlightened Universal reality. We practice living this interdependence for the sake of all beings.

You and I do not experience enlightenment alone. Why? Enlightenment is the experience of intimacy with all things. We are liberated from a belief that we are isolated entities. Liberation has many meanings. I am using it as freedom from the faulty perception which alienates us from ourselves, the human and Earth communities, and the way of the Universe. This is the heart of Eihei Dogen's teaching. He is one of the Zen ancestors who guides us in this book. Dogen (1200–1253) is the Japanese founder of the Soto Zen school I am trained in, practice and teach.

I imagine a variety of readers are perusing these pages. Perhaps you are curious about Zen. Maybe you've moved into or out of a tradition, or beyond formal religion entirely. Or maybe you already practice some version of Buddhist teachings on your own or with a formal group called a *sangha*. Do you have spiritual guidance or a community of support? Maybe you belong to more than one tradition as several of my students do. Impermanence keeps our lives on the move. Turning and being turned is the soul's continuous creative process. It is how humanity evolves.

AN OPENING

The energy of the cosmos is always moving. It is circling in our blood through the cells of these bodies. It moves the surging tides, the cycle of the seasons and the changes in human society. The way energy moves is both outward and inward. It is unfurling—opening and boundless. It is also enfolding—gathering inward into one point.

Take a breath. Gather air into your lungs. To inhale is enfolding. To exhale is the unfolding release. Can you feel how life energy is moving through your body right now? Pay attention. Perhaps a description pops up—"tingling" or maybe the sound of a hum, the feel of the heartbeat. Maybe the energy enfolds into a gasp or unfolds in a sigh. Wait a bit. The feeling of life energy as you inhale and exhale, enfolding and unfolding to become you, will change. Simply paying attention to life living through you is practice. "Our endless and proper work" says Mary Oliver. (2)

This book makes an assumption some scientists claim is unwarranted: the moving energies of the Universe are intentional, not random. Buddhists give a name to the generative source of all this energy. She is named The Mother of all Buddhas, *Prajna Paramita*. She is the source of awakening to our true nature. This true nature is buddha nature. The "All Good" of everything.

Anyone who realizes and lives the True nature of the Universe is a "buddha." The Universe intends our awakening. It invites us to evolve into who we truly are. We can choose to respond or not. To respond is our vow to practice realization. Just as humans ignore vows they make to each other, we can ignore the vow of the Universe to fulfill its purpose through us. Continued ignorance ("ig-noring") of who we are creates humanity's faulty perception. We do not see the magnificent human each of us actually is.

What does it mean to be magnificent? It simply means to be awake as your unique "magnification" of the Universe. Why did

5

the human species evolve? Consider our appearance as the Universe becoming ever more diverse in creative forms of Itself. Each day, I take refuge in the Universe and renew my vow to embody it. Religions use different names for the source. Ultimately, the ineffable source is nameless, formless.

The Universal source unfolds in diverse forms: toads, volcanoes, and many types of humans. Zen says these various forms are "not two," not separate; we are oneness. But because we *are* diverse, we magnify the one source in many ways. So Zen also says we are "not one." You, the dog barking outside, a person dying on the other side of the planet—each is a unique form of the boundless one Universe. Each being is both "not two and not one."

Have you had moments of intimately knowing both your oneness with all that is—a cloud in the sky, the earthworms, the people on the street—and simultaneously knowing the wonder of your particular existence? Many of us have such awakenings in childhood but have not found how to live them or understand what they ask of us. And so we wander through life…moving this way, exploring here and there, then turning back, confused.

Here are two sayings I came upon years ago that allude to such soul movements. The first is from the wizard Gandalf in Tolkien's *The Trilogy of the Rings*. He says: "Not all who wander are lost." The second is from a source I do not know: "You are already where any path can take you." Ponder these for a bit. Could both sayings be true for you?

By way of introducing myself to you, the reader, here is a brief description of how those two sayings have played out in my life. I turned through three major circles of change. The most recent began about twenty-five years ago—in the mid-1990s—when I chose formal training as a Zen Buddhist student. At that time, I was a college professor at a liberal arts Dominican college in Madison, Wisconsin. Previously, I had been studying and practicing Zen on my own. In 2010, after retiring from my college position, I was ordained a priest and teacher by Sojun Diane Martin in the Soto school of Zen Buddhism. Now, as one of Diane's dharma successors, I guide a women's sangha in Wisconsin. Two groups meet in Madison in my home. Another group of women in the Milwaukee area meet at the home of one of the members. We also meet online.

Prior to this most recent and still expanding circle came two other major cycles in my life. In each cycle, I sensed I was wandering but not lost. Somehow I trusted that I already was where any path can take me.

I did not feel lost during the first cycle of childhood and in my early years living in community and teaching as a Dominican sister. The path of the Dominican vocation was well marked. Our vows were lived to "contemplate and share with others the fruits of contemplation." This motto guided all choices and required everything of me. But the subsequent 25-year cycle mirrored the wandering many souls experience: searching beyond the limited view of one's upbringing, questioning social institutions, eventually feeling disorientation, loss, rage, grief.

During this time, the 1970s and '80s, I taught with other Dominicans in diverse parts of the United States. I was radicalized through several "turnings." From the roof of our convent in heart of Chicago, the sisters and I witnessed the city burn after Dr. Martin Luther King, Jr. was assassinated. My students turned me toward action for racial justice. They taught me my white privilege. In the Twin Cities, when the bishop tried to shut down our school, the last all-women's high school, I was liberated by the study of my oppression as female and moved into feminist action for women's full empowerment.

Then, while ministering in a Catholic Worker peace and justice house near nuclear warheads in Cheyenne, Wyoming, I co-led a group for disarmament. We prayed and demonstrated at the local nuclear weapons base and at the Pentagon.

Turning and Being Turned

Eventually, I realized that these various forms of violence and injustice are interconnected. They all arise out of an "original" sin: humanity's subjugation of and alienation from the Earth community of all beings.

Sisterhood was creative, affirmative, and vibrant, but the institutional Roman Church was not. So, during these years, I turned to the Christian mystics and the Zen path. My father introduced me to Teilhard de Chardin's view of the Universe grounded in science and evolutionary Christianity. Together, my mother and I explored Carl Jung's psychology and the Zen-infused writings of the radical Trappist monk Thomas Merton. My parents' soul longings moved in me. I kept expanding beyond traditional Christianity and questioned living as a public representative of the patriarchal Church.

Feeling caught in my cage of questions, I pushed my energy outward for ten years of that second cycle. My noble activist ideals spiraled as I climbed toward a perfection always out of reach. In my mid-40s, when the idealized tower collapsed, I fell into an abyss of not knowing. But while wandering in the classic "Dark Night," my soul did not feel lost. Instead, I felt helpless. I sought and found the support required for staying present in that dark time.

In 1984, I began work in Jungian analysis with Diane Martin. One April day, I experienced a world turned from darkness into radiance. The awakening was profound conversion. My suffering turned into the beginnings of freedom during the last years of the middle cycle. Deeper practice and painful choices were required. I continued the healing transformative work with Diane Martin.

My Dominican sisters lovingly supported my decision to leave the community. I moved to a new life teaching at a community college out West. The Rocky Mountains became a refuge. I also began a doctorate on philosophies of the soul. During the next four years I completed an interdisciplinary Ph.D. and accepted an appointment in the Philosophy Department of Edgewood college in Madison. The college is sponsored by the same Dominican congregation I grew up with. A full circle was completed. Formal Zen training with Diane and her sangha began.

Trusting that a Universal Presence lives through us is the offer of the Great Turning of evolution. It is personal and collective "conversion." Personal conversion can be a big, life-changing summersault or a more subtle pivoting. If we are attentive and responsive the heart*mind—one word in Chinese and Japanese languages—will move in ever expanding circles. Turning from ignorance and fear into awakening and trust is continuous. Continuous practice realization is who I am and also happens to be in the title of this book.

What Does This Handbook Offer?

Your book is designed according to the circle of practice realization taught by Eihei Dogen, the acclaimed 13th-century Zen master who founded Soto Zen in Japan. Each turn of Dogen's circle describes personal awakening within Universal awakening. Together, we turn from suffering into the healing of liberation. Recently deceased beloved world teacher, Thich Nhat Hanh, often said, "We inter-are." We are here to "awaken from the illusion of our separation."

Humankind could regress into increasing greed, hate, and delusion or evolve into more generosity, love, and wisdom. What we choose to pass on affects the future. When a choice is intentional, its energy resonates. This cause and effect is the basic understanding of "karma" in Zen. Thus, your personal future and our collective future from are "not two." You matter.

Turning and Being Turned

Dogen's teachings were brought from Japan to the United States in 1958 by one of his lineage heirs, Shunryu Suzuki Roshi. A "Roshi" is a venerable elder teacher recognized for fulfilling the imperative of passing on the Dharma and guiding students in the way of enlightenment. Shunryu founded the first Soto Zen Monastery in the West, Tassajara, in California. He also founded the San Francisco Zen Center where Diane Martin met him and began her Zen Buddhist training. When she moved to the Midwest, Diane also trained with Dainin Katagiri Roshi, who came from San Francisco to lead the Minneapolis Zen Center.

In 1990, Sojun Diane founded Udumbara Zen Center in Evanston, Illinois. Students from all over the country are drawn to study and practice with Diane Roshi. Udumbara is now a national network of sanghas led by Diane's students and Dharma successors.

Zen masters are often noted for a unique style. The Zen term *goruku* refers to the spontaneous sayings of a great teacher as they are heard by their students. Diane's style is spontaneous, startling and sometimes baffling. Her sayings, or "Roshi gems," are rich in paradox, humor, and metaphor. Diane uses classic Zen metaphors and also invents her own from contemporary culture. The samplings here are from my practice journals, as well as notes taken during Udumbara Sangha gatherings. They are not exact quotes. In the style of Ananda, the scribe of the historical Buddha, Guatama Shakyamuni, I preface these sayings with the caveat, "Thus have I heard."

Dogen also had a scribe, Kuon Ejo, who compiled Dharma hall discourses Dogen gave to his monks. The *Eihei Koroku, Dogen's Extensive Record* quoted below is the translation of Taigen Dan Leighton and Shohaku Okamura. (3)

Chapter Two of the book offers some brief passages from Dogen's *Extensive Record*. The *Extensive Record* is different from his other writings because we can sense the open rapport Dogen shared with his monks as he met with them day by day.

Chapter Three of this book connects a few of Diane's teachings with Dogen's circle. These are but small droplets of a streaming waterfall from Roshi Sojun Diane's oceanic heart*mind. I hope you will dive in.

Sophia Zen Sangha members are also co-creators of this handbook. Zen honors our relationship as "reciprocal becoming." My students show me how to view my small self through a wider lens. Reader, whether or not you and I ever meet on Earth or not, we are reciprocally becoming as you work with this book. In the great work of living our shared Universal essence, each of us is a unique "essential worker."

Sojun Diane offers us this invitation: *"May you have a constant pulsation of availability so that the Vow of the Universe—that all beings realize inherent enlightenment—may meet your personal vow to be a magnificent human being. This is our practice."*

WHY A TURNING CIRCLE?

The circle is used across cultures to represent cycles of human life, the natural world, and the evolving cosmos. It's easy to find many examples of cycles in dance and music—recall the "Circle of Life" in Disney's *Lion King* or Vivaldi's "Four Seasons." The Quaker hymn "Tis a Gift to Be Simple" asks us to come round to where we ought to be. The "Hokey Pokey" enacts enfolding into the center and unfolding outward as "you put your whole self in, put your whole self out... and turn yourself around." Humans do seem to feel "that's what it's all about."

The turning circle offers transformation. A Labyrinth exemplifies moving into the sacred center before returning, transformed, back to the outer world. The Sufi dancer begins with hands crossed over the heart then gradually unfurls arms and skirts to expand energy into the infinite. Designing a sacred circle or "mandala" of diverse energies held in harmony is a practice in many cultures. You will find suggestions for making a mandala in the Appendix. (4)

Descriptions of the circling of the small self within Universal Presence is the experience of many of the world's mystics. Consider this prayer: "O moving force of Wisdom, circling the wheel of the cosmos, encompassing all that is, praise to you! The structure of our hearts is influencing the structure of the cosmos." (5) To claim that your heart's choices *now* influence the planet and beyond is a teaching akin to karma.

From ancient rituals to contemporary insights of evolutionary consciousness called "The Great Turning" taught by Joanna Macy and others, the energy of the circle invites conversion. An ancient teaching of the Great Turning is the Wheel of Life, a mandala, taught by Gautama Shakyamuni, the historical Buddha. Diane has studied and taught the intricacies of the Wheel with our national Udumbara Sangha these past decades. The Wheel of Life portrays Universal archetypal energy. Our task is to be awake in its vibrational field—our life. We "betray the revolution," Diane says, quoting Rilke, by turning retrograde. We can transform the Wheel of Suffering into the Wheel of Dharma moment by moment.

Soto Zen's symbol is the open expanding circle called the *Enso* shown on the cover of this book. It represents your personal awakening within the vast, enlightening energy of the cosmos. The teachings "circulate throughout all time, in all lands...without neglecting anyone on the entire Earth..., saving all beings...demonstrating reality." (Dogen's Essay #53, *Buddha Sutras*.) (6)

There are many Buddhas throughout time and space besides the historical Buddha, Gautama Shakyamuni. Uncapitalized, "buddha" is the true nature of any and every being. The Buddha Way is not anthropocentric; nor do only sentient beings participate in awakening. Wetlands, viruses, metals, and mud— "*All beings are buddha nature,*" Dogen states in Essay #23, *Buddha Nature*. Not splitting transient matter from eternal spirit turns consciousness upside down for most non-indigenous Westerners.

To glimpse the wonder of "all beings are buddha nature," see the breathtaking paintings of Iwasaki Tsuneo in *Painting Enlightenment: Healing Visions of the Heart Sutra* by Zen teacher Paula Arai. She writes, "In painting an atom composed of buddhas [Iwasaki] is asserting that, in its most fundamental being, everything is made of wisdom and compassion energy; all forms are impulses to support interrelated ever-changing activity to diminish suffering." (7)

The circle of the way includes both the macro and micro structures of the universe. Everything is available for awakening into wholeness—how we release CO_2 emissions, how we care for each other during war, famine, or illness, how we stand for justice, how we love the next generation, one crying or giggling child at a time.

We could view the Earth's orbit around the sun as an example of a caring cosmos. If we were closer to the sun or farther away, Earth would not be a living planet. It could be incinerated or a rock of ice. If we can see compassion at work in the evolution of human life on this planet, perhaps we will trust it as the true nature of the human heart. Each human heart*mind has the capacity to be the cosmos consciously aware of itself.

Pause. Please look out the window. What did you see? A fully enlightened Buddha sees with human eyes and as the Universe aware of itself. Continuous practice realization offers your own heart's immensity. You have the potential to be the benevolence of the Universe.

There are four turnings in Dogen's design. In Essay #31, *Continuous Practice*, he names them aspiration, practice, enlightenment, and nirvana. Here is an excerpt:

> *On the great path of buddha ancestors there is always unsurpassable practice continuous and sustained. It forms the circle of the way and is never cut off. Between aspiration, practice, enlightenment and nirvana, there is not a moment's gap; continuous practice is the circle of the way...the power of this continuous practice confirms you as well as others. It means your practice affects the entire Earth and the entire sky in the ten directions...the moment when it is actualized is called now. This being so your continuous practice of this day is a seed of all buddhas and the practice of all buddhas.*

This handbook offers you entry into each turn of the circle through a selection of teachings from Dogen and from my teacher, Sojun Diane. Their sayings have the potential to turn one's consciousness around from ignorance to insight.

The 9th-century founder of the Soto school in China, Dongshan, describes this power in *Song of the Jewel Mirror Awareness*: "The meaning is not in the words yet a pivotal moment brings it forth." Your "inquiring impulse" is a turning point.

Just reading the words is not the same as allowing yourself to be turned around, inside out, and even upside down in contemplative silence. The book offers general suggestions but practice realizations are unique. Each of us is shaped by diverse conditionings of race, gender, age, culture, and many other variables. Recall that in our diversities, we are "not one," yet simultaneously we are one with all beings, past, present, and into the future. Simply put: your specific fears and struggles are not only yours. No one is suffering alone. And, while we are each responsible for choosing to awaken, no one becomes enlightened alone. Your practice includes a Universe of buddhas. As Dogen says above, "Your continuous practice of this day is the seed of all buddhas and the practice of all buddhas."

I encourage you to give your frontal lobe a rest as you spend time with this handbook. Let your thinking mind recede to allow space for the soul. The soul moves through an imaginal world of emotion, dreams, mythic, and archetypal energies. Your body is ensouled with these presences. The soul's realm is bigger than the rational consciousness which objectifies and labels your thinking.

You might come across terms you have not encountered before. This book includes basic explanations. I suggest letting a new term gradually reveal itself. Take an intuitive guess based on the context. *The Shambhala Dictionary of Buddhism and Zen* (Shambhala, Boston, 1991) is an excellent resource. You will also find definitions online.

Nevertheless, needing to know "What does this mean?" is not an expansive way of letting the teachings move in your whole self. Attaching to a meaning divides you from your soul, your body and the great Mystery that lives and moves within you and beyond. The soul realm connects your body and the material world with its spiritual source.

Consider the example of a rock. A rock is obviously a material object. Yet some religions call upon the divine as "our Rock." Matter (the physical rock) becomes the soul's portal to experiencing a Presence of unseen support. Whenever you come upon images and metaphors in the turning phrases, avoid analyzing them. Trust that a "pivotal moment" of intuitive wisdom will arise.

It takes time to discover what stillness will reveal. Have you heard the maxim "listen to your body"? Do you detect the dualistic split in this advice? Instead, let your body receive these teachings so awareness may arise *through* your body. Receive whatever turns up through your ensouled physical self.

We humans co-exist within the web of life on Earth. Dogen celebrates the teachings of bats and birds, of mountains, storms, and stars. All participate in and mirror your awakening. Each turn of the circle of the way is represented by a season and a time of day. Practice realization begins in the high noon of summer, then turns into autumn and evening's shadows. The bottom of the circle is the pitch dark of night, the cold stillness of winter. The circle then turns toward dawn with fresh breezes of spring. When we begin again, the process is familiar but not repetitive. Each circling offers greater depth of intimacy, more breadth of inclusivity.

Perhaps you have noticed that practice and realization are not discussed separately in this book. In Dogen's view, they are simultaneous. Our practice is turning into realization. Realization is how we are being turned into fuller, deeper practice.

Practicing today is not about pursuing realization in the future. Realization is not the goal of practice. Dogen states this in an essay appended to the *Shobogenzo, Fukazazengi*:

> *The zazen I speak of is not learning meditation. (It is) the practice realization of totally culminated enlightenment. The manifestation of ultimate reality…. If you want to be a person of suchness, practice suchness right away.*

As we practice in relative linear time, we are simultaneously present in Universal eternal time. Shunryu Suzuki put it very simply: "You are all perfect just the way you are and you could use a little improvement." (8) Simultaneously buddha nature and human nature. Both infinite and finite—that's you, that's each of us.

The flowering lotus is frequently used to represent enlighten-ment. Our flower's budding buddha self blooms in the messy mud of daily life. Diane likes to point out there is a seed pod resting within the flower. The image reinforces Dogen's words: "Your continuous practice of this day is the seed of all buddhas and the practice of all buddhas."(#31). While still in the seed's husk of ignorance, even deep in the mud, you are already a buddha! The Udumbara flower is the symbol of our national sangha. An Udumbara flower is said to bloom only once every 3,000 years. Practice realization means that the lotus is already blooming as you turn through the circle of the way. We need not wait 3,000 years.

Chapter One Notes

(1) For extensive and practical study of evolution's Great Turning, consult the Deep Time Network (dtnetwork.org). It offers live events and online programing concerning human-Earth-cosmos relationships and has diverse global participation. See also current online discussions of "Holomovement" connecting today's choices for evolution with David Bohm's book, *Wholeness and the Implicate Order*. (Routledge, London, 1980). Bohm's physics of an undivided, flowing Universe reveals a conscious cosmos.

(2) From "Yes! No!" in *White Pine: Poems and Prose Poems* by Mary Oliver, Beacon Press, Boston, 2005, p151.

(3) The *Eihei Koroku, Dogen's Extensive Record* quoted below is the translation of Taigen Dan Leighton and Shohaku Okamura. Wisdom Publications, Boston, 2004.

(4) A richly illustrated cross-cultural overview of the sacred circle can be found in *The Mystic Spiral: Journey of the Soul* by Jill Purce. Avon Books, New York, 1974.

(5) These words are often attributed to Hildegard of Bingen, an 11th-century Benedictine, but are not a direct quote according to Hildegard scholar Barbara Newman, June 2020.

(6) This passage and subsequent quotes of Dogen's essays are from *Treasury of the True Dharma: Zen Master Dogen's "Shobogenzo,"* edited by Kazuaki Tanahashi, Shambhala Publicans, Boston, 2010. There are various translations of the *Shobogenzo* available. I have chosen the Tanahashi translation for consistency and easier reference for the reader. Other editions and translations may have different titles and numbers for the essays or "fascicles." Consulting various translations can be illuminating.

The Shambhala Dictionary of Buddhism and Zen describes the *Shobogenzo* as "the most profound work in all of Zen literature." Shambhala Publications, Boston, 1991, p200.

(7) Shambhala Publications, Boston, 2019, p17.

(8) From *Zen Is Right Here*, David Chadwick, ed. Shambhala Publications, Boston, p1.

CHAPTER TWO

DOGEN'S CIRCLE: THE WAY OF CONTINUOUS PRACTICE REALIZATION

FOUR TURNINGS: ASPIRATION, PRACTICE, ENLIGHTENMENT, NIRVANA

As we saw in *Continuous Practice* (Essay #31), Dogen names the phases of the circle as aspiration, practice, enlightenment, and nirvana. In another essay, *Actualizing the Fundamental Point* translated as *Genjo Koan*, (Essay #3), he describes how to turn through each phase of the circle:

> *To study the way of enlightenment is to study the self. To study the self is to forget the self. To forget the self is to be actualized by myriad things. When actualized by myriad things, your body and mind as well as the bodies and minds of others drop away. No trace of enlightenment remains, and this no trace continues endlessly.*

We'll investigate *Aspiration* as our intention "to study the way of enlightenment." *Practice* is our ongoing "study of the self." Through practice, we realize we can "forget the self" of our delusions. The *Enlightened* True Self awakes as inter-being with myriad things. *Nirvana* is the full dropping away of separation from others into freedom and wholeness—right here midst the suffering world. Nirvana continues without adding "traces" of our small "me, myself and I." Big Universal Life is living Itself through us.

Aspiration: Intending to Study the Way

How does the aspiration to awaken arise? Since you are reading this book, perhaps it is stirring in you now. What is occurring in your life or in the world that calls to you? For many, aspiration begins as a felt unease, a restless dissatisfaction or alienation. The Sanskrit word *dukka* includes the whole gamut from a vague angst to a major crisis. It creates cycles of experience called *samsara*.

The first noble truth of the Buddhist path is the hard fact of suffering within human existence. This starting point is disturbing for some people. Yet, in the moment of actually facing dukka—a suffering that sometimes we can't even name—the aspiration for liberation can arise. Consider these few lines from *The Panther*, a poem by Rainer Maria Rilke:

> *His gaze, forever blocked by bars,/ is so exhausted it takes in nothing else. /*
> *All that exists for him are a thousand bars. / Beyond the thousand bars, no world...Now and again the veil over his pupils/ silently lifts.*
> *An image enters,/ pierces the numbness,/ and dies away in his heart.* (1)

The panther "now and again" knows he is trapped. He realizes he is cut off from his real life. We humans, however, have become expert in ignoring our freedom. We can accommodate so totally to constricted, faulty perceptions that we never aspire to break free. When tigers and lions, caged for years, are provided with a more natural, expansive habitat, often they are so thoroughly numbed they do not venture beyond the space of their former cage.

If our souls are not completely numbed when aspiration stirs the heart, the veil of ignorance will lift. Even for a moment, we can feel a space opening beyond the caged self. What is dissolving the veil? It is the liberating power of Wisdom. Zen calls this opening *kensho*.

Long before I heard of the Wisdom that brings light to our delusions—*Prajna Paramita* in Buddhist teachings—I felt the allurement of her presence in teachings about "Sophia." Sophia is Greek for divine Wisdom beyond all human understanding. She is praised in Judaic, Christian, and Islamic traditions. Wisdom Sophia is invoked by many Christian mystics including Hildegard, Thomas Merton, and Teilhard de Chardin. The Sophia teachings of Wisdom as our divine source have generally been sidelined in institutional Western religions. (2)

You will, however, find Prajna Paramita permeating Buddhist teaching and practice. In Dogen's Essay #30, *Suchness*, we read how she calls us to awaken:

> *Wisdom is transmitted to wisdom. Wisdom searches for wisdom and if you hear wisdom you trust and understand what you hear immediately. Wisdom is heard by wisdom. Although a person and wisdom are not acquainted with each other without exception the way is heard by wisdom.*

There is an echo of Dogen in Ecclesiasticus 6:26-29: "She will reveal herself to you. Once you hold her, do not abandon her. For

21

in the end you will find rest in her and she will take the form of joy in you."

Sensing our potential freedom from suffering, choosing to "get acquainted" with Wisdom and begin practice is offering one's intention.

The aspiration to awaken isn't alien to our nature. It is only dormant. A spark needing kindling.

Dogen emphasizes our buddha nature is innate. Ancient texts and modern teachers offer intriguing perspectives on buddha nature. (3)

The 4th century Yogacara Buddhist school provided a name for the mystery of buddha nature: *tathagata-garbha. Tathagata* is Sanskrit for "suchness." The word is also translated as the "thusness" of everything. These words attempt to signify the ultimate or Absolute reality of all things. *Garbha* is the suchness "seed," the buddha embryo.

The Dominican mystic Meister Eckhart (1260-1329) used the word "Isness" to preach this radical, non-dual message to the common folk of Rhineland, Germany. He used traditional theistic language because belief in God was the common view. Eckhart taught: "If you were to ask 'What is God? I reply: Isness. Where there is Isness, there God is.*"*

Eckhart also uses the metaphor of the seed for our true nature: "The seed of God is in us. Now the seed of a pear tree grows into a pear tree and a hazel seed grows into a hazel tree; a seed of God grows into God." (4)

Try closing your eyes. Imagine the cosmos as an infinite womb. It is dark and seems empty yet it is fertile. Energy for birthing an evolving Universe is pouring forth. Yogacara scholars envision this womb as a storehouse called *alaya vijnana*. The *alaya* is the boundless shared womb of all buddha being. The embryos—or seeds—are waiting to mature. The concept of alaya could be compared to Jung's collective unconscious. Here the other "seeds" lie dormant or are coming to consciousness in our dreams as the collective myths and archetypal energies unfold. Buddha nature in embryo is ready within to awaken. Ready to stir as energy for your aspiration.

As a young Dominican sister, I encountered the writings of Meister Eckhart but I did not understand them. Now I see how similar Eckhart is to Dogen. Eckhart's *Circle of the Way* or *Via* mirrors Dogen's Circle. Aspiration is called the *Via Positiva* by my medieval Dominican brother. It is the arising of your sacred "Isness."

Please pause to take in the "tremendum" of this offer. Your most intimate essence is eternal and infinite. You and I and all beings are within the vast womb of the cosmos expressing the "Isness" of reality. The womb is not void but full of interdependent, dynamic creativity. No wonder this Wisdom Womb, Prajna Paramita, is celebrated as the Mother of all buddhas.

All beings, including the insentient, are buddha nature. The entire interdependent cosmos, this Earth and its web of life, is suchness. Nothing is excluded. Everything, no matter how horrible it is from a human perspective, is supporting our personal intention to awaken. "Suchness can be shocking," Diane once told me. No matter what arises in the "Earth Emergency," we are invited to receive the care that is always available. What is that care? It is Wisdom expressed as compassion.

Another word for aspiration is "vow." Some vows are offered informally in private. Formal vows are public, intended to be lived in the context of societal or religious institutions. However you intend to study the process of awakening, note that the teachings gathered here have been offered to students who formally requested them. They participate within a sangha guided by a recognized heir of the Soto Zen lineage, traceable back to China and India to the historical Buddha, Gautama Shakamuni. Not everyone in a sangha publicly professes the vows of a *bodhisattva*. A *bodhisattva* is an enlightening being who aspires to wake up for the sake of all beings. Sangha members—beginners to elders—continuously deepen their original intention.

There are, of course, informal practitioners who do not join a sangha or identify as Buddhist. As Shunryu Suzuki said, "You should find your own way and you should know what kind of practice you have right now." (5)

However, taking specific teachings—such as those offered here—out of the context this rich tradition can be confusing and misleading. For example, the famous quote "Everyday mind is the way" could lead someone to the false conclusion that in Zen, your attitude to life can be simply "whatever." Teachings can be misconstrued to permit morally questionable behavior. There is an ethics inherent in practice realization that Buddhist teachers and students honor when they receive the precepts and endeavor to actualize them in their thoughts, words and deeds. (6)

Diane consistently reminds her students: "Every state has an ethical imperative." How do we realize that imperative? How do we train to offer an appropriate response? We begin a diligent practice of the study of the self, the next turn of the circle.

Aspiration

Nirvana

Practice

Enlightenment

Dogen's Circle

Take a look at the design of Dogen's circle. Aspiration is positioned at the top of the circle, signifying noon. It is honored as the bright energy of summer. But no matter the time or place we can always express the heart's aspiration to practice. Each time we step into the *zendo*—our practice place—Sophia Zen students and I are mindful to embody our intention to practice. We don't wander in, scanning the scene. We stand upright in silence at the threshold, bring our palms together to make a small bow and step in. Then we walk with dignity toward the altar. Bowing before the meditation cushion, we acknowledge the Universe's vow of support for our awakening. Those little cushions represent all existences through time and space. They are making practice possible.

Next, we each turn around to offer a third bow in gratitude for the sangha community. Lots of bowing! Sometimes we laugh, "When in doubt, bow!" Putting palms together before my heart, I inhale. Then, exhaling, I incline my head and shoulders. This simple bow, called *gassho*, embodies my aspiration to awaken with all beings.

Practice: Studying and Forgetting the Self

Many people are conditioned to ignore or avoid a deep study of their inner lives. Primal ignorance is a restraining energy. In Roshi Diane's turning phrases, you will encounter its imaginal personification, *Yama*. This name means "The Resister." *Yama* is not satanic. Buddhist teachings do not have the concept of original sin. There is not an entity named "Satan" or a separate "God" entity.

Yama signifies the force that alienates us from our original wholeness. Human conditioning into the faulty perceptions of dualistic thinking begins early. The human identity set-up is based on oppositions called the "the eight worldly dharmas":

25

- gain v. loss
- pleasure v. pain
- success v. failure
- praise v. shame

Adapting to these perceptions of self-identity shapes us to function in human society. We learn to compete; we strive to avoid failure. But this built-in dualism cuts us off from our birthright of true "enough-ness" and goodness. Besides, when we gain anything, we then fear its loss. Today's praise is impermanent; blame or shame could show up tomorrow. That's the "set-up" of dualistic thinking.

We need lots of practice recognizing how original ignorance puts blinders on our wholeness. *Yama*'s devious tricksters are called the *maras*. Here's an example. I may be conditioned to believe that needing help makes me inadequate, even a failure. This "mara message" sneaks into my thinking. I don't see the set-up that tricks me into jumping from one polarity to the opposite. If I cling to what the culture believes is a successful self, automatically the opposite, a failed self, is constructed. The opposites depend on each other.

Much of Zen's study of the self is the practice of recognizing how dualistic either-or patterns obstruct our true nature. They keep us caught in a deluded sense of self. We are like those newly freed animals who accommodate to their culturally constructed identity "cage" and cannot see their natural, spacious habitat.

The most intimate practice for studying the self is our daily *zazen*. (The practice of zazen is discussed in Chapter Five.) Zazen trains us for continuous practice during the day. Study of the self in dialogue with a teacher (called *dokusan* or a practice interview) and in sangha is emphasized in our school.

Dogen's study of the self must be deeper than intellectual understanding. It requires the courage to "forget" or let go of ingrained habits. It takes ongoing commitment. I often ask students to pause during the day to detect within: "Am I practicing now?"

Personal relationships, local, national and global issues, the life of planet—nothing is excluded in the study of the self. I once heard a radio host saying he needed to "zen out." Escapism is the opposite of this practice. We "zen in" to everything—including what we'd prefer to avoid. Our study and practice of the way includes "the whole works" as Katagiri Roshi liked to say.

Maturing as skillful students of the self is gradual. Patient, ongoing discernment of ethical skillful means is key. Skillful means can include therapy and other forms of support. Shakyamuni Buddha was once asked by Ananda if loving friends were part of practicing the way. He was told that loving friends are the whole of practicing the way. With such warm-hearted words to his dear cousin, I think Shakyamuni was summing up his teaching of interdependent co-arising. Our practice friends need not be close by and might not be human. Consider a special tree or animal companion.

A Soto Zen motto advises, "Take considerable care." I read "considerable care" using the Latin *considere*. *Con* means "together" and *sidere* means "with the stars." The care is already given—the Universe intends our awakening. How do we "take" its care? We take refuge in its three treasures: Buddha, Dharma, and Sangha. In *Returning to Silence: Zen Practice in Daily Life*, Katagiri Roshi describes these treasures:

> *Buddha is the Universe and Dharma is the teaching from the Universe and Sangha is the group of people who make the Universe and its teaching alive in their lives.* (7)

27

Living in harmony within the Universe is a succinct summation of how practice turns into realization. We do this by discerning when our lives are not in harmony, not aligned with the Wisdom source of the Universe.

How do we learn to recognize when we are out of cosmic tune? Just like fine-tuning the sound as we listen to music, we note a shift into static. We feel this static—the suffering of *dukka*—most intimately in our bodies. We can sense we're off center and have wobbled out of tune to lean toward one opposing worldly dharma or another. The mind dial moves—clinging to praise or pushing away shame; to denying pain and grasping for pleasure, for example.

To be a clear, upright channel, catch the tendency to lean toward any of those eight opposing dualistic dharmas. This may sound obvious but not so! We are so attached to our favorite mental soundtracks, we don't even realize we are being pulled toward afflictive states. Once a student smiled as she admitted to the sangha, "I work so hard to make my life so difficult!" So first we must see the suffering state we're caught in. Perfectionism? Jealousy? Anxiety? Resentment? There are many ways the eight worldly dharmas show up.

Next we practice letting it go. We release our identity grip to open as a clear channel for the natural way the Universe is working.

We expand our "bandwidth"—as another student put it. Our life eventually becomes the resonance of cosmic harmony. We choose to be the "flow through" of energies for an awake planetary community. Tibetan Buddhists have a wonderful saying for this freedom: "AH HO! Relax in the natural awareness of Great True Nature."

Three necessities support us. The first is "Great Faith." Faith means trust in your innate goodness, buddha nature. Faith helps you withstand the inner skeptic, the mara message "you are inadequate, unworthy" or "sitting practice is a waste of time" or any one of a variety of the mara insinuations of resistance.

"Great Courage," the second necessity, is required to let go of the familiar and predictable refrains of self-talk. We have believed these messages for so long we assume they are true. We believe that an identity label IS me! It takes courage to drop these messages. They have been like relentless "ear worms" for years. As Wisdom grows, we recognize habitual self-talk more quickly—in a nanosecond instead of a week. A gentle sense of humor helps.

We become skilled in the third necessity: the "Great Doubt" of these deeply programed beliefs. The "don't-know mind" of Great Doubt gives us pause. Here is the opening for the Wisdom beyond human knowing, Prajna Paramita, to arise. Wisdom's heart is the offer of compassion. We begin choosing to be loving, whole, and free over and over. One day we find ourselves saying, "This practice really does work!"

There are stories of Zen monks realizing enlightenment at the sound of a pebble hitting bamboo. But, as Diane once remarked, "their awakening was no doubt preceded by thirty years of patient cultivation." Practice realization is the work of a lifetime of faith, courage, and the doubt of old patterns.

Recently Diane shared a little poem Katagiri Roshi wrote in his last years:

> *I want to thank you, my American students,*
> *for making me strip off layer after layer*
> *of cultural skins.*

Stripping off the layers of our conditioning requires tenderness. As Mark Twain famously said, *"Life is like an onion. We let go of layer after layer and sometimes we weep."*

Autumn is a letting-go season. There is a turn from studying into forgetting the self. The leaves of the old identity tree drop off moment to moment. Finally, the branches of the self-structure bend in the wind and are stripped bare. The brightness of day turns into liminal twilight. Zen ritual embodies this turning of our practice when we prepare for a full prostration: knees drop to the ground, the body curves over. We are ready to be turned upside down.

Enlightenment

An ecologist guiding hikers pauses before a log resting on the forest floor. The hikers may assume, "Oh, that tree is dead." But the ecologist understands how nature conceals new life forms in the dark: life and death, "not two." The log that appears dead is actually filled with creative energy. It is burgeoning with life. Perhaps the tree may support the forest as it decays even more than when fully flourishing. Nature's cycle relies on the dying process. Compost in your garden is breaking apart old forms as they deteriorate.

On a larger scale, the Earth cycles through major "die offs," such as the previous five major extinctions. The destructive forces of the cosmos clear the way for new possibility. The death of a star releases an immense burst of radiant energy. Sixty-five million years ago, asteroids flaming through the atmosphere, meteors, and volcanic eruptions resulted in the climatic changes of the fifth massive extinction, including the disappearance of dinosaurs.

The next phase in the epic of evolution has been described as "The Dazzling Abundance." Early mammals and other life forms, waiting for their chance, emerged out of hiding. Patricia Gordon writes that there was "never a time in the 4.5 billion years of the Creative Planet's existence with as many species of life as at this time." (8)

What "dinosauric" structures—in your life and in society—do you sense are now collapsing? If worldwide institutions structured for the powerful few placed over "the others" collapse, will new forms of human consciousness emerge?

Another well-known example of old forms transmuting into new life is the caterpillar cocooning itself. It relentlessly consumes its own energy to the point of exhaustion. Scientists now report that the dropped-off "mush" of the former caterpillar contains the imaginal cells of the butterfly's transformation. A poster I saw once sums up the total turn-about required in this phase of the circle: "It's the end of the world!" cried the caterpillar. "It's just the beginning," whispers the butterfly.

I am writing during a worldwide pandemic and political instability. Recently, I read an essay in the magazine section of *The New York Times* by Sam Anderson entitled "The Truth about Cocoons." (9) He describes how society's "normal" structures are turning to mush:

> *How do we even begin to process all of this – this cataclysm that is happening. Simultaneously in slow motion all at once. On distant continents and inside our own cells...acts of internal self-destruction and rebuilding; subtle shifts and whole revolutions."* A cocoon is actually a chrysalis, *"a hard shell that was inside the caterpillar's body the whole time. From the ancient Greek 'chrysos' – 'gold' – a golden envelope of internal self-destruction. In order to expose the chrysalis, the caterpillar just has to slough off its chubby outer layer."*

> Anderson asks, *"Is a butterfly's life any better than a caterpillar's? Was all that suffering worth it?"*

Even with faith in our enlightenment, we fear what is beyond human knowing. In the *Prajna Paramita Sutra in 8,000 Lines*, there is a vivid description of not knowing whether entering the dark will be "worth it." Picture yourself standing in total darkness on the edge of a cliff. You know you must surrender your current certainties in order to turn into greater life. You are willing but you are also terrified. Sense yourself standing on your particular "cliff edge" in loving compassion. The sutra says you hold two "parachutes"—one hand holds the parachute of Wisdom ready to shine through the darkness; the other hand holds the skillful means you have learned to practice. You step off that cliff and leap into the unknown. (10)

From the perspective of the ego, enlightenment could just as well be "endarkenment." Dogen tells you: "Your body and mind as well as the bodies and mind of others drop away." Note the words "your" and "others." Dogen is not saying the ego is destroyed. Rather, the self that clings to a "you" separate from "others" drops away. That belief no longer controls your experience. Enlightenment transforms our awareness of being alive. Our interdependent co-arising existence awakes.

An early *Mahayana* text, the *Lankavantara Sutra*, describes this turning about of consciousness:

> *When the mind ceases to discriminate and there is only perfect and love-filled imagelessness, then an inscrutable turning about will take place in the inmost consciousness and one will have attained self-realization of Noble Wisdom. That is the highest Prajna Paramita.* (11)

The "inscrutable turning about" of each person's self-consciousness can never be fully described, but mystics of all traditions testify that it must be endured in trust. What was bright and sure at noon as we entered the circle cannot be seen at midnight. We no longer depend upon the light of ordinary consciousness when awareness of the infinite breaks us open.

There is a NASA photo on my wall calendar. It shows a supernova in a galaxy near our Milky Way. Where did this supernova come from? Scientists now know that the supernova was created from dwarf stars. The separate, impermanent dwarf "form" is gone, not its essence. Energy is now free for transformation by a boundless, creative, cosmos. Enlightenment releases the fullness of the Universal Self.

The ego does not see death as radiant or accept it as a place of growth. Patiently waiting within endarkenment requires tenderness. So often we forget to give ourselves compassion. I was inspired by the following experience of enlightenment's radiance within darkness. It is offered by Zenju Earthlyn Manuel in her book, *The Way of Tenderness: Awakening Through Race, Sexuality and Gender.* (12) The event occurred during zazen at night on a retreat:

> *... We were all a part of the dark. In the darkness I was a part of everyone and everything whether I accepted it or not...In the dark I recognized life without all of the things we impose on it and upon each other ...When I turned toward my heart in the silence, I entered a kind of tenderness that was not sore, not wounded but powerfully present...Complete tenderness almost wiped me out. And perhaps it does wipe 'you' out – the you that suffers so, that 'you' unaligned with the Earth body...The way of tenderness appears on its own. It comes when the events of your life have rendered you silent and have sat you in a corner and there is nothing left to do.* (15-28)

The anguish of the world is our shared womb of fertile darkness. We might not consider endarkenment as tender. But that is what Mother Prajna Paramita offers to her child: compassion beyond our expectations.

In practice, we embody the turn into enlightenment as we complete a full prostration. The head touches the Earth; simultaneously we lift the palms of our hands above the bowed head, seeing nothing. We hold them open and still. As we wait, we are like dead wood or cold stone. The chant *Song of the Jewel Mirror Awareness* describes being turned into awakened life by power beyond our own: "The wooden man begins to sing, the stone woman gets up to dance."

Nirvana

Nirvana is enlightenment's actualization. Bodhisattvas actualize their awakening for the liberation and healing of world. Saving all beings is not the ego's project. The person free to live beyond the ego's identity project becomes a spacious, free conduit for Universal Life.

Nirvana is technically translated as "cessation." What ceases? The mechanism of self-making ceases so that our True Life energy now moves freely in selfless spontaneity through one's unique gifts.

Dogen's description in *Genjo Koan*:

> *When actualized by the myriad things your body and mind as well as the bodies and minds of others drop away. No trace of enlightenment remains, and this no trace continues endlessly.*

In Sophia Zen Sangha we pondered a poem of nirvana actualized in a 13th-century nun. Her name was Chiyono. Under a full moon, Chiyono was carrying water from a well: "The bottom of the bucket fell out of that woman of humble birth;/the pale moon of dawn/is caught in the rain puddles." (13)

Chiyono's enlightenment "moon" was shining in only her personal "bucket." Then it broke open to flow out into the world, leaving no ego trace.

The circle of the way turns from the dark of winter to the dawn of spring. The buddha seed blossoms in the world free of traces of self-achievement. Sounds lovely, doesn't it? However, the famous image of a monk entering the marketplace with "bliss-bestowing hands" can be oversimplified.

Koan #89 is more direct: "*Follow the spring breeze into the scars of the burning…*" (14)

Here is the vow to actualize nirvana in a scarred and wounded world. A lotus blooming in the fire is an image showing samsara's suffering is the exact place as nirvana's awakening. After awakening, we will meet the juncture of potential samara or potential nirvana. Which reality will we choose to enact? The seeing power of Prajna Paramita reveals the fire as radiant compassion. A choice to embody love opens the heart. "She brings light so that all fear may be forsaken." (*Hymn to the Perfection of Wisdom.*) Maturing in wisdom, compassion, and skillful means is a continuous circling. When I forget, I renew my aspiration to awaken. A new turn into practice begins.

In the *Extensive Record,* Dogen told his monks: "There is the principle of the way that we must make one mistake after another." (#88) By that, I think he meant we will all make the "mis-take" of splitting samsara and nirvana. We forget our lotus flower blooms in the fire of suffering, rooted in the mud of the human predicament.

So instead of trying to "zen out," we renew our intention. As we exit the sangha zendo we bow and re-enter the zendo of the world. We choose liberation moment by moment. We are circling the way without clinging to merit, the "traces" of self-making. That would be like trying to keep spring's blossoms in a private homemade vase. We keep moving as we are actualized by the changing experiences of this precious human life.

A SAMPLING OF DOGEN'S TURNING PHRASES

The passages below are from Dogen's *Extensive Record*.

Dogen is speaking informally. He knows his monks are familiar with the imaginal, intuitive way Zen often is taught. To us, these phrases can be disconcerting. Give the images time to resonate without trying to figure out an intellectual meaning. Metaphors work at deep levels even if we do not grasp their allusions. Dogen's writing has its own poetic logic. Give his approach a try. In the next chapter, you will discover how Diane's words bring the same circle of practice realization alive with her contemporary insights.

Aspiration

BUDDHA NATURE: *Become a seedling of the Buddha Way.* (#139)

ENGAGE THE WAY: *Great Assembly, we have already received a human body difficult to receive and we have already encountered the Buddha Dharma difficult to encounter. We should engage the Way as if extinguishing flames on our head.* (#480)

HOLDING THE JEWEL: *Everyone without exception holds the jewel that glows in the night. Unless we turn the light within to illuminate the self, how can we hold close the jewel when we are lost in the outlying countryside?* (#282)

GREAT COMPASSION: *The oceanic vow of great compassion has no shore or limit and saves living beings with release from the harbor of suffering.* (#320)

INTENTION'S MAGNANIMOUS ENERGY: *Our wondrous existence is most excellent...How could there be arising and perishing as our magnanimous energy pierces the heavens? (#286)*

LIFE AND DEATH: *Thoroughly investigate life in order to understand death. Letting go and taking hold of life and death depends on your refinement. (#311)*

DOGEN'S WAY: *I Eihei simply wish that you all disport and play freely with spiritual penetration...that you all trust what your hands cannot hold. (#266)*

DO NOT STOP: *The fire boy comes seeking fire. With complete dedication do not stop when you have only seen the smoke. (#299)*

Practice

DESIGNING A BUDDHA: *Have no designs on becoming a buddha. If you practice Zen by designing a buddha, Buddha becomes increasingly estranged. (#338)*

JUST SITTING: *Just sitting is the Zen practice of dropping body and mind. Mind cannot objectify it, thinking cannot describe it. Just step back and carry on and avoid offending anyone you face. (#337)*

THINK BEYOND THINKING: *Sit on your cushion and think beyond thinking. Play vividly and energetically but don't be fooled by any demonic spirits...laugh and destroy the net of delusion. (#279)*

NOT EASY: *You should know that studying the way is not at all easy...Search for the fiery lotus in the water of mind. Study this. (#291)*

DIFFERENTIATE: *A crow alights on a black horse; within differences there is sameness.* (#307)

MUD: *Where there is much mud, the Buddha is large.* (#140)

JUMPING CLEAR: *Become capable practitioners...After time scoop up toads and jelly fish in your net and put your minds to the work of jumping clear...immobile sitting is boundless."* (#322)

EAT BREAKFAST: *Karmic consciousness is endless, with nothing fundamentally to rely on including not others, not self, not sentient beings, and not causes or conditions. Although this is so, eating breakfast comes first.* (#306)

TODAY: *Realization is just sitting zazen. Do not pass your days and nights in vain. Human life is impermanent; how can we wait for some other time?* (#319)

Enlightenment

NO REGRETS: *A snowflake falls on a fiery furnace. The black dragon's jewel is behind the straw sandals. Who would regret the moon in the vast sky?* (#409)

GREATEST COLD: *If this greatest cold does not penetrate into our bones, how will the fragrance of the plum blossoms permeate the entire world?* (#34)

EMPTY YOUR HEART: *Body and mind dropped off--how do we discern their absence? The sage empties out his own heart. The ten thousand things are nothing other than my own production. At this very moment, how is it?* (#501)

SOMERSAULT: *My teacher Rujing turned a somersault and the bottom of the bucket dropped out. The school of Dongshan (i.e., Soto) entrusted this ancient teacher and now it has come to us.* (#276)

ILLUMINATION: *Cherish the dropping away of body and mind. Eyes like lightning illuminate the Milky Way.* (#272)

STILLNESS: *Not letting in any view of outside, not letting out any view of inside...complete the ten thousand affairs—Maha Prajna Paramita.* (#333)

BLACK GLOW: *On the night Tathagata (Shakyamuni, the historical Buddha) completed true awakening...all the various beings in the 3000 worlds smiled...Here the black glow of a single monk's staff is pure.* (#506)

FLOWER IN THE COLD: *A single plum flower in the cold, with fragrant heart blossoming, calls for the arising of spring in the emptiness of the cauldron of ages.* (#481)

Nirvana

MIST CLEARS: *The night mist clears, scrubbed clean by the dawn wind.* (#266)

DAWN: *Do you want to understand the principle I am teaching? (pausing) The five petaled flower opens in the timeless spring. The single circle of the moon is white in the dawn sky.* (#279)

GOING BEYOND: *People who have fully attained transcend (their) seeing and go beyond hearing and freshly join with others...uphold the ancient path, no longer sinking into debilitating activities.* (#285)

Live Paradox: *Be solitary without dependency...Be like the moon stamped on the water, flowing but not flowing. Like the wind in the sky, move but do not move.* (#316)

Mind: *Consciousness is not perception...Mind is not the ability to think. Do you want to understand in detail why it is like this? (pausing) Amid spring rain, spring wind and spring grasses and trees are yellow nightingales, earthworms and toads.* (#317)

Delight: *Delusion and enlightenment retain their places; the spring wind is delighted to belong amid the cold plum blossoms.* (#308)

No Traces: *The function before the empty eon is used without leaving traces and the mind seal tucked under the arm is empty.* (#264)

No Seeking: *Who would complain that spring radiance does not seek after anything. Exactly thus, exactly now all sense fields are perfect wisdom.* (#152)

Returning to Life: *Dropping our bodies while crossing over, we can return to life...Freely observe and follow the tracks of the birds in the sky.* (#450)

Notes to Chapter Two

(1) The full poem, published in 1902, is in various anthologies. Please check online.

(2) For a compendium of worldwide Sophia teachings, including contemporary scientific insights, see *Sophia-Maria: A Holistic Vision of Creation* by Thomas Schipflinger, trans. James Morgante, Samuel Weiser, INC, York Beach, Maine, 1998.

(3) See Essay #23 "Buddha Nature." Also consider Sallie B. King's excellent analysis of the term in *Buddha Nature,* State University of New York Press, Albany, NY, 1991.

(4) *Meditations with Meister Eckhart.* Matt Fox, Bear and Company, Rochester, VT, 1983, 12.

(5) *Zen Mind, Beginner's Mind*, edited by Trudy Dixon, Weatherhill, New York, 1986, p74.

(6) For contemporary ethical applications see *The Eightfold Path*, a collection of essays by contemporary Soto Zen women teachers published by Temple Ground Press, Olympia WA, 2016. My students found it very helpful.

(7) Shambhala Publications, Boston, 1988, p78.

(8) See *The Epic of Evolution—A Version of the Universe Story* by Patricia Gordon. http//rainforests.org.su/deep-eco/patricia_gordon, 2003, as well as *The Great Story* (www.thegreatstory.org), which includes my essay, *A Zen Way into the Universe.*

(9) May 24, 2020, p10-12.

(10) Translated by Edward Conze, Four Seasons Foundation, Bolinas, CA, 1973, Ch. 20, #13-14.

(11) From *The Lankavatara Sutra*, translated by D.T. Suzuki, edited by Dwight Goddard, Monkfish Book Publishing Company, Rhinebeck, NY, p85.

(12) Wisdom Publications, Boston, 2015.

(13) *The Hidden Lamp: Stories from Twenty-Five Centuries of Women's Awakening.* Edited by Florence Caplow and Susan Moon, Wisdom Publications, Boston, p97.

(14) *The Book of Serenity: One Hundred Zen Dialogues*, translated and introduced by Thomas Cleary, Shambhala Publications, Boston, 2005.

CHAPTER THREE

TURNING PHRASES OF SOJUN DIANE MARTIN

Blue will not tell me.
Green just walks into a tree.
Today I give up—then-
Red beats a new heart trail
Sparks a thousand ways to meet.
—Diane Martin's poem, Fall 2006

W hen working with this selection of Diane's teachings, select a quiet environment and sit in a comfortable, alert posture. If possible, give yourself meditative time beforehand. Read one or a couple of phrases slowly—either silently or in a whisper to yourself. Zen and other religious traditions often do things in threes, e.g., three breaths, three bells, three bows. There's a reason why.

At first, we may not be centered and mindful when we begin reading a phrase. Then we may not fully be present while we are reading it. Re-focus if you are distracted. Finally, it can be helpful to wait in silence before you decide to move to another phrase. Let your contemplative inquiry with the selected phrases come to a natural ending.

I encourage you to use a practice journal. (There are suggestions for using a practice journal in Chapter Five.) Let yourself write freely about whatever arose. It could be a bodily feeling, a memory, an image, or a recollection of another teaching.

Questions or confusions may show up. I remember an image Diane came up with for our questions: *They can work like magnets for attracting future insights.*

One immediate way to honor a charged teaching is to print it out as a flash card. Hold it when you next meditate or post it in your home where it will catch your attention and invite a mindful pause. A friend suggested making your own deck of cards. Perhaps include phrases that make no sense now but could be revealing later. Of course, there are other ways besides writing to express and embody how a phrase has touched you. Suggestions for other ways to use the turning phrases are in Chapter Five of this handbook.

Eventually you will discover your own methods.

Your practice realization process cannot be rushed. If a phrase is stirring in your heart, honor your experience. As Diane once told us: *Pull over to the side of the road.* When the Deep Mind is engaged, the phrase can resonate and work its way into your life.

ASPIRATION
The Turn into Awakening

Diane uses the Sanskrit term *"bodhicitta"* for aspiration. *"Bodhi"* means enlightened; *"citta"* means mind. In aspiring, we are actually initiating our realization of awakening.

AWE: *Are you ready to become a juggler of the impossible? This practice should appropriately awe the ego.*

LIVE FRESH: *Teach the ego to live fresh. The ego will need to give up its fixed personality.*

Turning Phrases of Sojun Diane Martin

Problem/Solution: *This practice is based on the wholeness of reality. Be ready to discover that the problem is also the source of the solution.*

You are Many: *In Buddhist cosmology, there are no "others" to save. The beings in you are numberless. This is the bodhisattva path of Universal awakening.*

Depletion: *When we feel worn out and depleted is a good time to commit to the Way. There is a creative side to depletion.*

Potential: *We have unlimited potential. Don't be afraid of your true capacity. Place yourself at the edge of your life.*

Silent Illumination: *Soto is a silent illumination school. This does not mean indulgence in trance, dullness, bliss states. We are silent to discover the rapport between the illumination of insight and the settling of stopping.*

Aspiration is not a Goal: *In Soto, we don't go anywhere.*

Bowing: *Our bows mean receptivity to the activity of the Universe.*

Practicing is Personal, but Not Private: *Our personal liberation liberates the whole. This is the teaching of interdependent co-arising.*

Compassion: *The Universal field of awakening is expressed as compassion.*

Give the Frontal Lobe a Rest: *Don't give too much credence to the intellect. If it has all the votes you lose other ways— more immediate ways—of realizing the jewel.*

The Heart is Everywhere: *The basic, basic music of the Universe is ours. The heart of the matter is everywhere.*

Turning and Being Turned

Don't Underestimate Yourself: *We can allow much more depth than we might guess. To do this work we need our whole selves on board.*

Shoulds: *Your greatest imperative: fulfill your enlightenment! Examine all other "shoulds."*

Karma: *We cannot avoid our karma. So we might as well live it in vow.*

Trust: *Trust Prajna Paramita will do the work through you. She is illumination, open to seeing stars in the daylight.*

See Your Caughtness: *It will require a lot of getting caught for freer aspects of mind to be revealed. A whole new arrangement is possible!*

You are not In Charge: *Get beyond the "I" pronoun. You are not in charge of your true life. Things exert themselves; things realize us.*

What Do You Value?: *Value life more than habits. Practice will help you liberate the continuum of a habit-based personality.*

84,000 States: *Ancient Pali monks proposed that humans have 84,000 delusion states. Therefore, we have 84,000 ways to wake up.*

Honor Yourself: *Don't diminish your personal suffering as small compared to big collective suffering. Catch the sadism in such thinking.*

Cocooning: *Shakyamuni Buddha's image of suffering is a cocoon. We keep spinning our cocoons until, like the caterpillar, we die of exhaustion.*

Turning Phrases of Sojun Diane Martin

EVOLVE: *Honor the evolutionary attainment of the always open mind.*

SOTO SCHOOL: *We are a totality school. Everything arising is necessary.*

SEE THE EDGE: *What is the edge of your growth? Feel your gravity rocket of resistance drop away.*

YOUR BODY: *Before the body's intelligence was usurped, Wisdom's seeing energy flowed through the body.*

LIMITS: *The ego often dishonors the body's limits. Learn to revere what goes against the ego's habits.*

RESTING: *What familiar sense of self do you like to rest on? The free body rests on nothing!*

ACCEPT BEING ALIVE: *We learn to tolerate existential angst—the basic tension of being alive is always present.*

REJECTION: *Where do I put the experiences the ego does not want? Everything wants to return for wholeness.*

BE READY FOR GEYSERS: *The unconditioned uses broken-open cracks in the self. Be ready for geysers of insights. Be a conduit for Prajna Paramita. She will arise!*

DEPTH: *Going deep is always the way when things aren't working on the surface. This is being loyal to the generative source.*

WILL POWER: *Enlightenment is not an expression of the will.*

NEVER ARRIVING: *The Way is not organized around arrival. Keep asking —what is right in front of me that I can't see?*

BODILY INSTINCTS: *Be prepared for the bodily instinct to panic. See the ego's preference for comfy spirituality.*

Turning and Being Turned

PROGRESS: *Drop your spiritual history. Erase the tracks of progress and give up striving to make more tracks. The ego doesn't even realize it's on the train.*

MYSTICISM: *Honor your natural capacity for mystical states. Spacing out in the void is "Zen sickness," not mysticism.*

SPONTANEITY: *Don't resist all the upsurges of the Universe as it tries to come to us. Spontaneity is a serious word in Zen.*

UNFORESEEN GIFTS: *Sitting gives space for all kinds of unforeseen eruptions—personal, ancestral, collective. These are presents from the infinite that want to be opened.*

WHOLENESS: *If we could tolerate both the light of consciousness and the vast, dark matter and energy of mystery, what an expansive Universe we'd be living in!*

THE VOWED SELF: *The vowed self must not collude with the ego's drive for attainment. Hold the circle open. Convert the ego's mastery drive to not closing.*

BIRTHING BUDDHA NATURE: *We are both the womb and the embryo. Crack open the egg. The chick is way past due!*

JOY IS ALWAYS READY: *Joy is mentioned an equal number of times as suffering in the classical texts. Invoke at will a joyful mind.*

PRACTICE:
Turning Moment to Moment

"WHO" IS STUDYING THE SELF? *Who is practicing? Who is avoiding mystery? Keep asking 'who' questions.*

"WHAT" QUESTIONS: *What beliefs are creating my life? What does the discursive mind say to and about me?*

THINKING: *Thoughts are brain secretions.*

ASSUMPTIONS: *See the assumptions that push the stream of becoming. Relinquish connecting the dots the self wants.*

SOME SKILLFUL MEANS: *Lean into an experience. Aerate and expand the experience. Open space to loosen the grip on experience.*

STATES: *There is no preferred religious state. We are not our states. Therefore, we need to exercise Great Doubt to keep us safe from our own labels.*

RELATIVE AND ABSOLUTE: *Buddha nature is impermanent in its relative expression. The Absolute immutable Self is eternal but not static.*

OBSERVER'S POWER: *See the process of creating a self "set-up." Use the Heisenberg principle: the observer changes the experiment.*

NOT DOING: *The teaching of not doing is tough. We can't imagine there is vitality in not doing.*

GOODNESS: *Be aware if your ultimate aliveness is being corralled into the archetype of doing good.*

SELF-EVALUATION: *Don't over-evaluate the evaluator. This is not the discernment of authentic study of the self.*

DISCERNMENT: *Discrimination is not the skill of discernment. Discriminating separates. Use discernment skills in order see separation.*

GET OUT OF SELF-HATE: *Never move into anything anywhere that is trying to bring you down. Be a "first responder" for liberation. Act fast!*

STOP AND SEE: *Practice the "stopping and seeing" skill to stay with and see into the depths of your experience as your own Zen teacher.*

CUTTING THROUGH: *Know how to use your wisdom sword to break open the entangled self knot. We cut through in order to open up space.*

DESIGNATING MIND: *Stay with raw life and avoid labels for boxing the self.*

THE SELF IS A CONSTRUCTION: *With practice, we can see the house of self the ego is building as it happens. Stop as soon as you realize your thoughts are constructing an "I." See the "housebuilder" at work.*

EMPTINESS: *The Mahayana views emptiness as each and all beings contained in all others, permeating boundlessly.*

IMPERMANENCE: *With ease, just let birth and death happen, then allow a new birth. Cut the chain of clinging to becoming something, someone.*

EQUANIMITY: *Equanimity holds and includes all. Equanimity doesn't mind what comes up.*

Turning Phrases of Sojun Diane Martin

No Comment: *Go deeper to find the place where you abide with no commentary. There practice occurs.*

Perfection: *No one can be alive and free when hypervigilant.*

Trickster: *The trickster Mara can make us believe that we're being mindful and awake when it's really the opposite—scrupulosity. Don't shackle Buddhist teachings in karmic conditioning. The biggest threat to the trickster is when we see through its predictable set-ups. Practice pattern recognition.*

Teflon Principle: *Whatever is in your brain pan, let it slip out. Use the Teflon principle.*

Multiple Eyes: *Practice requires multiple eyes. If we usually prefer to see only one position, we can only use our energy one way. The octopus moves eight limbs, using multiple eyes.*

The Choo-Choo Train of Becoming: *In the momentum of becoming, discern which skill is needed. An abrupt stop of the train, uncoupling the cars? Kindly braking to step off the train?*

Humor: *Mara can't stand a good laugh.*

Feelings: *Ask: What is my attitude toward this feeling? Am I willing to let it stand there stark-naked? Do I resist? Do I split off from my own humanness?*

Emotional Weather: *There is nothing wrong or right about emotional weather. Embody the non-grasping of feelings which arise.*

Free From Continuity: *Can you enjoy being at loose ends? Allow the ego to feel this homelessness?*

Quick Thinking Can Miss A Lot: *Acknowledge the superficiality of grabbing an idea, going to the next, avoiding depth.*

Differentiation: *See what we devalue and what we raise up. Differentiate and be willing to use anything and everything for practicing.*

Liberation: *All good liberation moves are double. They take life—cut, stop, put down. They give life—open, flow, receive.*

Vastness: *We belittle the sky by looking through a pipe. Stand clear of the closing door.*

Dynamic Becoming: *Are you like the pigeon who wears down her beak pushing the same reinforcement button? Stay loyal to the future's dynamic becoming.*

Ways We Get Caught: *We ignore retrograde. We go to sleep, blank out. Or we want a quick clear answer.*

Collective Suffering: *All our personal suffering is collective. All beings exist in the deep mind. We are committed to the whole body of reality.*

Boredom: *Boredom is incredibly rich. It is a stepping point into infinity. Stay diligently bored!*

Barriers: *Keep your Zen sword sharp each day, spot your barriers. A dull prajna sword can't cut through a tomato.*

Conversion: *Investigate each state as you experience it. See what has not been converted. The self must be turned around. Everything needs conversion, including the idealistic religious personality.*

Zazen: *Your zazen is not yours. Be on the edge of mystery all the time. Let zazen do zazen.*

Turning Phrases of Sojun Diane Martin

Drop Pros and Cons: *If we hold two things in our mind, know the trickster will pick out our favorite.*

Doubt the Trickster: *If something is not working, the trickster may say "do it more, do it harder." Turn that around.*

Fixed Self: *Giving up a fixed self is giving up something that isn't.*

Let Soul Space Move: *When stuckness is taking up too much space in the psyche, send it to daycare.*

Skill in the Moment: *Catch the self as it coagulates moment by moment.*

Same Old Tune: *You can always tell if a stuck state is defending itself because it sings the same tune over and over. Spot derivative refrains from the old self without comment.*

Don't React: *The ego can't stand non-reactivity. The ego fears the potential death of going beyond its script.*

Erasure Mind: *There are ways our capacity for realization could be erased: blanking the mind, shutting down, refusing to ask, "What am I leaving out?"*

Score-boarding: *See your addiction to measurement. We like score-boarding and avoid not knowing. True progress is renouncing the neon scoreboard sign.*

Difficult Relationships: *Our ultimate cohabitation is with all life. See relationships in this context. "Not one, not two" is non-local subjectivity.*

Where are You Going?: *Reality is everywhere. Why do we think we are not at that source?*

TURNING AND BEING TURNED

EMPTINESS AS POSITIVE: *Watch language of emptiness as loss. Emptiness is positive inter-permeating.*

THE BODY: *We don't need to pay better attention to the body. The body is already in a state of attention.*

MOVING MIND: *Authentic movement requires relinquishing goals, a need for closure and assuming what we already know.*

EMPTINESS: *We cannot observe emptiness. Emptiness is the way we realize nonduality. It liberates samsara.*

HEART OPENING: *When we awaken to the reality that has not been processed by the ego centered mind, compassion is already present. There is no "before and after."*

COMPASSION DEPENDS ON NOTHING: *Spontaneous heart opening is the non-dependent arising of the unconditioned.*

SATURATION: *This culture resists saturation. We grab the quick surface response. Instead, stay with what is and allow deeper saturation. Wait. Allow the experience to tell you.*

INTERRUPT: *If you interrupt your habitual processes in the service of awakening, you will have immediate results.*

AMNESIA: *Convenient forgetting, ignoring a situation, shutting down is amnesia, a mind-corrupting principle. It short-circuits dynamic becoming.*

ZIPPER PRACTICE: *Allow opposites to come forward and intersect. Use dualities as dharma doors.*

DROP REFERENCE POINTS: *Our practice is complete, non-referential ease. Reference points are harbors which close us in. Sink into a deeper ocean.*

GO DEEP AND WIDE: *If we provide space everything is waiting to arise. Prajna Paramita will come in.*

WILD RIVER: *We are all agoraphobic, afraid of our freedom. Send your kayak down the wild river that disappears...always moving, always going beyond.*

ENLIGHTENMENT
Turning Into the Dark

TO THE ROOTS: *We are working on the roots of unresolved karmic sufferings avoided in our study of the self. In the darkness they will exhaust themselves.*

SUPERIOR PRINCIPLE: *The dark is the superior principle. It is the empty absolute negation of what human consciousness grasps.*

ENDARKENMENT: *The endarkenment of deep space or the oceanic dark is always available. Here we cannot know what the Absolute is doing.*

NO SPLITTING: *The Buddha Way does not split the dark of ignorance and the light of wisdom.*

DON'T KNOW MIND: *Keep unknowing open for liberation beyond your understanding.*

SATORI AND KENSHO: *Satori is restructuring of the whole self. Kensho is a temporary opening, like the Red Sea parting.*

TOTAL BEING: *That which is aware of fear is not afraid. Don't try to tell Total Being what to do!*

How Long?: *We do not need make an extended retreat for radiance to shine in the dark. A few moments of holy waiting in "don't know mind" can be revelatory.*

Awareness: *In the dark, give up your "doing" energy. It is the job of radiant awareness to melt delusion. Allow the dark to do its work.*

Groundlessness: *Walk in emptiness with no predictable cobblestones in place. Break the bridge as you cross it.*

Moment: *Ask: "Am I in moment?" Then also ask, "Am I in radical moment?" Know Totality's arriving. Don't move for 17 pulsations.*

Realization's Unceasingness: *In the dark we might feel the growth capacity is frozen. Endure stillness and trust; accept realization's unceasingness.*

Great Death: *We all resist our next stage of growth. The "Great Death" continues over and over, deepening and more demanding.*

Prajna: *The prajna voice speaks things the ego would never think of. The True Eye cannot think. It knows.*

No Signage: *Stop any road building for planning or control -- no signage even when the ego begs: "Where are my signs when I need them?"*

Cataclysm: *Don't try to make a meaning out of cataclysm. Stand upright in the middle of it.*

Dark Field: *The Universe resides in darkness. 95% is dark energy and dark matter. So much is going on in the dark field.*

Feel the Restraint: *Yama is the ultimate primal restraint on freedom. The name "Yama" literally means "restraint."*

Turning Phrases of Sojun Diane Martin

Don't Stay in Hell: *We can stretch through all the forces of hell without staying in hell. Grief work need not impair our strength to take on Yama.*

Grieving in the Dark: *Honor universal grief. Universal grief can dissolve clinging to a personal grief experience.*

Endurance: *Slog it out. The coal is the diamond. Everything is redeemable. There is a jewel in the garbage.*

Totality: *Let all reality be itself. Just so. Reality illuminating itself. Thusness.*

Drop Doing: *For the ego to realize darkness as non-doing is shocking. Non-doing is no effort, no fixing. This is not apathy. Apathy is a near enemy of non-doing.*

The Crucible: *Emptiness is the providing power of darkness. It is the crucible of allowing things to be rearranged. Rely on the dark.*

Keep Going: *Let yourself go through many transformations. Be suspicious of quick clarity.*

Energy Just Is: *Stay in the alchemical vessel of a situation. Allow a felt sense. The energies of forms just are. Meet them without naming.*

Transmute Old Forms: *The dragon (i.e., cosmic power) is where the energies of forms transmute into formlessness. Get inside the dragon's mouth but not chewed up.*

The Fire Dragon's Jaws: *The "jaws" are an open matrix where opposing forces are taken on. As we withstand the fire, opposites can transmute and dualities are free of dualism.*

Bottomlessness: *The ego wants to get to the bottom of things, a closure, a solution. Be bottomlessness.*

Turning and Being Turned

Negative Learning: *Fifty percent of all learning is negative. Working with the negative is a highly regarded Buddhist practice.*

Pranja Eye: *Wisdom sees what is revealed and what is concealed in darkness. Wisdom sees aspects of the unenlightened mind.*

We are All Wounded: *What are you like when you are inside your deepest wound? In what ways are you carrying your wound behind your back? How is your seeing power obscured by your wound?*

Two Woundings: *There are two wounds: the karmic experience and also the identity built around the wound.*

Bloom in the Fire: *The lotus blooms in the fire. Only when we recognize we are suffering will we accept the freedom to stop creating a suffering self.*

Your Power: *How powerful will you choose to be? Take Yama's sword and use it on Yama.*

Ending Patterns of Suffering: *If we don't end an abusive relationship with a pattern of suffering, Yama — the force of ignorance — will persist until the end of time.*

Claim the Power of Vow: *Inscribe your vows for liberation in your liver, in your brain synapses. Get off the wheel of suffering.*

Barriers: *Know how you encounter fear, negativity, and other barriers to sitting within endarkenment. The barrier is a dharma gate.*

Let Awareness Hold You: *In Zen, we do not progress by reaching outward toward attainment but ever deeper in respectful intimacy. Awareness holds us.*

IN THE DARK WOMB: *Trust you are the gestating fetus in the growth toward fuller and fuller awakening.*

ALLEGIANCE: *Feel into the transfer of your allegiance from suffering to liberation. The energy of the transfer liberates.*

EGO'S DEFEAT: *Every expansion of the self will feel like a defeat to the ego. There's no free lunch in the dharma.*

DEFEAT MARA: *Mara, Yama's minion, demanded of Shakyamuni, "Who do you think you are to be enlightened?" We too need to be ready for this attack. Don't permit self-destruction.*

THE PROMISE: *The "never-fear-always-present promise:" Our vow to remove obstructions will be fulfilled and will make space for the Universal heart*mind to arise.*

RISING TO LIFE: *Prajna Paramita is like the mother whale whose baby starts to sink when it's born. The mother swims under and lifts the baby whale to the air over and over until the little one learns to breathe.*

NIRVANA
Being Turned Within Myriad Beings

BE THE LIGHT: *We get up from the cushion to enter the world. To be the place from which illumination comes. Shakyamuni's last reported words to us: "Make of yourself a Light."*

VOW: *Your vow engages you to the limit of reality. Trust the moment will provide if we do our work.*

GOING BEYOND: *Post-enlightenment practice requires going beyond your current understanding. The indeterminant is the* *only constant. Allow new creative forms and formless creativity.*

The Actualized Self: *The radial, radiant self is not bound by time and space.*

Continuous Practice: *"Always moving" is a key Buddhist principle. Liberation never stops moving.*

Be Available: *When the Dharma of generative life breaks open, it keeps moving. Be available for enlivenment.*

Jewels Scatter: *There is no fixed reference point for the self to be in the empty field; the jewels are free to scatter in multidimensional energies.*

Natural Doing: *When movement flows naturally underneath agendas, bare awareness is taking care of all doings. Give over to naturalness as animals do.*

Autonomy: *Liberate any prohibition of the natural, authentic self. This is the path of autonomy and appropriate response.*

Your Agency: *How does your agency continue to get captured post awakening? Why does the injured self keep coming up? Know how, when, why.*

The Full Body: *Solitude and stillness support full body well-being. We are changing the teachings into our bodies.*

Birth and Death: *Deepen complete acceptance of birth and death. Attain the mind that is always letting go. All we are giving up is the show that does not really work!*

Ongoing Re-Arrangement: *We are re-arranging ourselves as human beings in dynamic expressiveness.*

See the Layers: *Train to access many layers at a glance. Even a child can see all the detailed layers of the Grand Canyon.*

TURNING PHRASES OF SOJUN DIANE MARTIN

THE STAGE OF THE PERSON: *Dogen's "Stage of the Person" is the union of personal self-actualization and Universal accomplishment.*

REVERBERATING LIBERATION: *After awakening, we continue to pierce through the "skin" of our views of ourselves. As self-obsession is continuously liberated, "7 buddhas back" are reverberating.*

LIBERATE EVERYTHING: *We have many lovely talents but can still misuse our real treasure. Liberate everything of the old self.*

UNENCUMBERED ACTIVITY: *What is the point of effort geared to achieving anything, including realization, except to reinforce the self? Unencumbered activity is a Prajna Paramita term.*

UNCERTAINTY: *The fact that we never grasp ultimate certainty is good. Why? The mind is always seeking ways to shift into other variations of certainty schemes.*

KARMIC RESIDUE: *When karmic residue is spotted, rejoice! Yama's power can be in every nook and cranny. Those who refuse to fall for it can be free.*

CONTINUOUS PRACTICE: *Continuous mistakes are for continuous practice of awakening. Go back into the messiness without shame.*

LIVE EVERYTHING: *Allow the archetypal energies to move, be the complete orchestra. The Universe makes the symphony.*

NO NEED FOR EFFORTING: *Let us flow free on the stream in our canoes. Throw away our paddles!*

INTEGRITY: *Rilke writes, "Beauty is born of just bearable terror." Consider this rewording: Integrity is born of just bearable awareness.*

Turning and Being Turned

The Membrane of Relative and Absolute: *Pick up one thread of relative thinking and the whole will be there. Work the membrane of the one and the many.*

Birthing the Self: *With awareness, keep the cervix of birthing of the Self supple. Skeptical doubt is holding back the ongoing process of liberation and entrapping the child.*

Gratitude: *Don't just push ahead or eat your heavenly cookies of gratification. Gratitude is different.*

Enlightenment in Delusion: *Delusion is never "over." Trust enlightenment never functions without delusion.*

Progress: *There's a price to be paid for progress. We give up attachment to what we've already learned. We all resist our next stage of growth.*

Greater Freedom: *The freedom zone of Prajna Paramita is boundless. When a practice "raft" has supported movements then let it go.*

Mastery: *If you believe in mastery you are using the raft on dry land. Drop it and open beyond. Dogen calls this "desporting freely."*

Always Awake: *A complete Zen person is always awake—not easily fooled and able to shift states easily. Always awake means habits are not allowed to take hold in their former state.*

Pure Awareness: *We must leave the threshold of the attaining mind. This is purification of the whole process. Devotion to pure awareness is our primary practice.*

Kensho Depth: *We can go deeper and deeper into a kensho. We can keep learning from one of long ago.*

Turning Phrases of Sojun Diane Martin

Relativized Ego: *The ego can function if it knows its place. Leave darkness as darkness and do not interfere with what is.*

No Self: *No self is beyond and different from the individuated self. Enjoy the individuated self and let it wave goodbye from the harbor of the ocean.*

Bodhisattva Work: *Saving all beings is the huge practice of human recovery. Know this as <u>the</u> suffering, not merely ours.*

Claim Joy: *The trickster carries disbelief in the natural fountain of joy.*

Popcorn Metaphor: *When all conditions are aligned popping open happens all at once, like popcorn. No struggle. Let the dharma percolate, like popcorn in a bag.*

Play: *Enjoy your life. Celebrate allowing yourself to be the center of your own play.*

Never Finished: *After seeing the jewel we redo the skandhas over and over as we sit on our flowing lotus.*

Swim the Ocean: *Wake up! We have to swim around the world tonight. Who will we meet? It depends on how well we swim.*

We'll Stop Bouncing!: *When the habitual self is gone, our various ideals and self-attacks no longer bounce us about on the trampoline mind. The spell is broken.*

Regression: *If we do not keep deepening our practice, regression is inevitable. Just be awake in the process.*

Personality: *Cut off a fixed personality that wants to help others. Personalities don't save beings!*

TURNING AND BEING TURNED

ETHICS OF REALIZATION: *Every state has an ethical imperative. Therefore ask "where am I positioning myself in this moment?"*

TURNING ABOUT: *"Pavritti" inversions of consciousness occur often. A "summersault" can be long and slow or a quick pivot.*

MERIT: *Be free of gaining mind but don't forbid delight in your own giving nature. The bodhisattva distributes merit to all beings.*

YOU ARE VAST: *The normal appraisal of what we experience as self is pitifully tiny. Perhaps 10 experiences out of 10 billion.*

ZAZEN: *At a certain point zazen will do itself. All we do is simply protect it. Zazen rolls on like the ocean.*

HELPING OTHERS: *We must continuously liberate our own suffering. Then we help others automatically.*

FRUITION: *Belief in an endpoint is a trap. Appreciating fruition is not resting on the laurels of gaining mind.*

DYNAMIC FRUITION: *As karmic states are weakened, there is less interference. Awareness shines through faster and more fully. Fruition is dynamic.*

GOING ON: *Continue realizing beyond realization. Carry the experience of indeterminacy.*

THE REPEAT: *Of course, states will continue to repeat. Learn freedom in the middle of the repeat. Never underestimate the power of the delusional mind.*

Turning Phrases of Sojun Diane Martin

KARMIC RESULTS: *As you mature see karmic results before they happen. Shakyamuni did.*

EMPTINESS AS RECONSTRUCTIVE: *Dogen's view of emptiness is preeminently reconstructive. The 10,000 things, inner and outer, are no self coming forth as Self.*

EVOLUTION: *Be one with the evolutionary drive of the Universe. Human flowering is already given by the Universe.*

CHAPTER FOUR

LIVING THE CIRCLE
OF THE WAY

YOUR ORDINARY LIFE,
MYSTERIOUSLY PROFOUND

Your life is the circle of the way, yet its circling is impossible to calculate or measure. Can you describe the wonder of being alive? Can you calculate how much you are worth? Can you measure where "you" begin and where "you" end? The circle symbol in Zen is open. Practice realization expands from the energy of an invisible fundamental point. Including everything, excluding nothing. Hmmm…what comes to mind for you that feels shocking or repulsive? What feels glorious or tender? As Diane taught in the last chapter, "the beings in you are numberless" and "the heart of the matter is everywhere."

Every life is a profound mystery, like a *koan*. In Japanese, "ko" can mean "ordinary." "An" can mean profundity. Whether I am a grasshopper, a virus, or a human, I am a koan—simultaneously profound and ordinary. Dogen coined the term as *Genjo Koan* (Essay #3). "*Gen*" means a great secret and "*jo*" means immediately present. (1)

Thus the immediate present moment of your experience—an ache in your back as you read, for example—is both apparent and hidden. The mysteriously profound is concealed in the ordinary.

"Big things pose as little things," Diane teaches. Try putting these insights together to say something like, "While I am obviously immediately present, my indescribable vast life is a mysterious secret. My true life includes everyone and everything." This means you are and are not the center of your life. The fundamental point is everywhere. As early Christian mystics often said, "God is a circle. The circumference is nowhere, and the center is everywhere."

Well and good. Pretty amazing. But how do I live this, you may ask. How am I going to get enlightened? It's a common question. Recall how Dogen refuses to separate your ordinary daily practice from realizing enlightenment. Can you detect a problem with a question about someone "getting" enlightened?

The Heart Sutra proclaims "there is nothing to attain." (See Appendix.) Why? The foundational Buddhist teaching of no-self means we inter-are. We are not separate individuals who either get or do not get a "thing" called enlightenment. Rather, limitless enlightening activity pervades the Universe. Our personal practice realization is two-fold: recovering our original enlightenment and then cultivating it in practice.

During the spring of 2020, Diane taught a Zoom class on the Wheel of Life for the national Udumbara Sangha. George Floyd had just been murdered in Minneapolis by the police. Scarring covering this country's deep wound of systemic racism was ripped open. The wound was enflamed. The Twin Cities and other cities were burning.

A Dharma sister and friend who lives in Minneapolis told us, "Practice like your hair is on fire—because it is!" Enlightened activity begins like this—recognizing ourselves within the world's suffering and making the intention for liberation. Diane then reminded the sangha: "Negative forces want us to stay stuck in our woundedness. If we are not tending to the formative conditions for our enlightened activity, what are we doing?" We all sat silent.

I suggest the first formative condition is not to fan the flames of suffering. Then the healing and compassion of Wisdom's glow may shine through us in any specific painful situation. Waking up means we realize when we are at the juncture of samsara and nirvana. Then we have a choice: which fire will blaze in our hearts—more flames of suffering or the healing warmth of love? Which fire do we tend? Whenever you tend the bright radiance you are, there is enlightening activity.

Dogen gave us a description of eight enlightened activities in Essay #84, *Awakenings of Great Beings*, which he wrote for his monks in the year of his death, 1253. The list is based on advice given by Shakyamuni Buddha. Each one of these awakenings offers support for living your circle of the way: for your aspiration, your study and forgetting of the self, your trust in the radiant dark, and your actualization of awakening.

"First, have few desires.

Second, know how much is enough.

Third, enjoy serenity in seclusion.

Fourth, engage in wholesome practices with diligent effort.

Fifth, maintain mindfulness and right thought.

Sixth, abide in the dharma without being confused; have stability in meditation.

Seventh, cultivate wisdom. Without wisdom you will not attain liberation.

Eighth, leave behind scattered mind and hollow discussions. Know that each enlightened activity includes all of the others; thus we are encouraged in sixty-four awakenings."

These teachings are encouragements, not commands. Each of us will hear them in the context of personal conditioning and specific situations. Each of us uniquely aspires to recover the buddha seed of original enlightenment, cultivates it and waits within for our dark ground to open as a fresh blossom unique in all the world.

Enlightening energies shine out through your physical body as it stands now in this world. It has no limits in the ten directions and the three times. You are personally "being turned" by the Great Turning's awakening energy. The Dharma Wheel reverses the retrograde energy of collective suffering. Energies of greed, hate, and delusion permeate the world with fear. Each choice to awaken transforms them into generosity, love, and wisdom.

Consider this slightly adapted hymn to Prajna Paramita, the Mother of all buddhas. The full hymn is the Appendix. Pause before reading to inquire: What particular fear or distress do I hold now?

> *Homage to the Fullness of Wisdom...most excellent are her works. She brings light so that all fear and distress may be forsaken and disperses the gloom and darkness of delusion. She herself is your seeing power. She clearly knows the true nature of all beings for she does not stray away from it. The Fullness of Wisdom of the Buddhas sets in motion the Wheel of Dharma.*

The short version: A wise, loving response is always possible. Pass it on. It will transform the world.

LIVING THE CIRCLE OF THE WAY

ENCOURAGEMENTS

THE FIRST ENCOURAGEMENT: HONOR YOURSELF

Your practice realization matters. It is a gift that "keeps on giving," as the saying goes. The pebble in the pond sends ripples beyond itself. The intention to awake—or the refusal to do so—reverberates beyond this life in physical form. I re-read Dogen's essay *Jijuyu Zammai* when I need encouragement. The full text is in the Appendix. Here are a few of the lines:

> Since these enlightened ones in their turn enter into the way of imperceptible mutual assistance, the person in zazen without fail casts off body and mind, severs the heretofore disordered and defiled thoughts and views emanating from his discriminating consciousness, conforms totally in himself to the genuine Buddha Dharma, and assists universally in performing the work of Buddhas at each of the various places the Buddha-tathagatas teach, that are as infinitely numberless as the smallest atom particles.

> Yet such things are not mingled in the perceptions of one sitting in zazen, because this occurs in the stillness of samadhi beyond human artifice, and is in itself realization. If practice and realization were two different stages as ordinary people consider them to be, the one sitting in zazen and things should perceive each other. To be associated with perceptions is not the mark of realization, because the mark of realization is to be beyond such illusions.

> ...when even just one person, at one time, sits in zazen, they become imperceptibly one with each of all the myriad things, and permeate completely all time...

71

Turning and Being Turned

Even if all Buddhas of the ten directions, as innumerable
as the sands of the Ganges, exert their strength and with
the Buddhas' wisdom try to measure the merit of one
person's zazen, they will not be able to fully comprehend
it.

Such words of encouragement are rather overwhelming. They seem impossible. Remember, we do not become enlightened by ourselves. Our dedication to the way is honorable in and of itself. Try not to compare yourself with anyone else.

In my years of teaching, whether in the classroom or in the zendo, I've often witnessed how students dishonor themselves. To dishonor the self, or to aggrandize the self by placing oneself above another, is a symptom of hierarchical dualism. Hierarchical dualistic consciousness has dominated much of our species since the Neolithic Revolution about 12,000 years ago.

In reading Elinor W. Gadon's book about the evolution of human culture, *The Once and Future Goddess: A Symbol for Our Time* (2), I was surprised to learn that this construction of thinking was precipitated by the movement of peoples due to climate change. Put *very* simply, prior to the Neolithic Revolution, migratory gatherers and hunters in the northern hemisphere lived within clans, in caves. When the glaciers melted, that way of life was disrupted. Gradually these hunters and gatherers became breeders of animals, settling down in villages and towns. They organized a hierarchical division of labor that was no longer based on interrelatedness with the natural world.

What the West now calls "civilization" was the turn to actively intervening instead of being at one with the Earth as the ground of being. In the Book of Genesis (written much later), we read the story of God's proclamation to Noah: "All the animals, birds, and fish will live in fear of you. They are all placed under your power." (3)

72

New tools, defensive weapons and walls against "other" groups turned collective living into hierarchies of power. Previous Earth-based circular societies became linear. The ruler was typically the dominant male. Everyone "below" was subjected to him and all could be considered his property: his wife, children, soldiers, workers, and slaves taken in war. Animals became objects, not kin. The land became a resource, not a living organism.

This thinking persists. A tree is now under a Department of Natural Resources. The grocery store label on the plastic package says "bacon" or "beef tenderloin." The actual tree or pig or cow is invisible as a subject. It became an object for our use.

While indigenous peoples have courageously sustained an Earth-based communal consciousness, after 12,000 years of ranking our species on top of every other being, hierarchy predominates. Dualism splits diverse humans into various forms of "insiders" or "outsiders." Hierarchical dualism dominates most all social structures. Perhaps in this turn into climate change and a new awareness of our interdependence, we will evolve beyond the belief system that has caused untold suffering. There can be the re-volution into the Great Turning—the vision we are honoring in this book.

Hierarchical dualism is worldwide, but it is also intimately personal. It shows up consistently in comparison mind and self-diminishment mind (or self-inflation mind). Women are very often conditioned into self-diminishment thinking. Have you ever noticed how women tend to apologize for no reason? In the grocery aisle, the laundromat, or a narrow hallway, women may say, "I'm sorry" for just being present.

Probably, I recognize this afflictive state because of my early woundedness as a religious sister in the male-controlled hierarchical Roman Catholic Church. Nonetheless, hierarchical dualism infects our shared consciousness of race, class, abilities, nationalities, as well as gender and sexual identities. It works in the plethora of ways we humans use our differences to compare and rank each other.

From cradle to grave, systemic ranking (hierarchy) and splitting (dualism) permeate the foundation of human institutions such as family, education, politics and economics. The construction is insidious in its double whammy. First is duality, the splitting between self and others, us and them. Then hierarchy ranks and privileges one side above the other. In our earliest years, identity is formed by the bias of hierarchical dualism. Unconsciously and consciously, it works to legitimize fear, greed, hate, and other forms of oppression—including Eco-cide.

The suffering that results will not end in law courts or political reform. Laws against hate speech and justice reforms are necessary and important, but only a beginning. Structures of human consciousness that promote oppression—including an ingrained anthropocentrism—are deeply rooted in the self that believes it is separate and positioned as either above or below "others."

The Zen phrase "cutting through the root" refers to the profound transformation required. It is radically inverting this process of self-making to collapse those structures.

The *Lankavatara Sutra*, cited in Chapter 2, teaches:

> *"When the error of all discrimination is realized the turning about takes place within deepest consciousness. Mind, thus emancipated, enters into perfect self-realization of Noble Wisdom" (39-40). Also "there is no trace of habit energy generated by erroneous conception..." (30) What remains is the true essential nature of things—the Suchness of Reality (36).*

When any one of us deconstructs a hierarchical dualistic mind state, the consequences will be huge. One of my students recently proclaimed such a liberation kensho. She said "I am done with that cruel self which has tormented me with perfectionism all my life! I am *done!*" Her personal liberation expands because the energy constrained in affliction for decades is now transformed, released beyond for others. Her self-liberation is personal but it is not private. It is now in synch with Universal energy.

In one of the turning phrases, Diane says, "Liberating our own suffering helps others automatically." How is this possible? The afflictive energy that was locked into a grip onto "my" suffering is now free. It sets in motion the Wheel of Dharma.

Do you recall the story of that little Dutch boy who held back the surging sea with his single finger plugging the dike? Let's turn the story upside down. I now like to imagine him as the little ego desperately trying to stop the immense surge of the power of the All Good Universe. You can pull the plug of the ego's grip. The courage to do such work means feeling how you tighten around your particular conditioning. Releasing it is resting in the truth of your true nature—more spacious than any constraining identity.

As you study and forget your small self, become familiar with the unique ways your conditioning sets up a suffering self. Investigate kindly. That ego has pushed you into building a dike, if you will, to protect you from fear of your full immense possibility. It has served you the best it could. Practice realization discloses the limits and biases of its faulty perceptions.

Comparison mind is deeply ingrained in consciousness— from body shape and skin color to health, income, abilities, politics, and more. What examples of measuring stand out for you? Any ranking or labeling of the self—better or worse, successful or failing—can inhibit trust in your basic goodness and in your capacity to express it. Your enlightenment process is therefore subverted.

Please accept your true nobility. Great Faith is necessary for us all because the wounds of hierarchical dualism infect the collective human body. This is true whether I am oppressing others or the one being oppressed. Often we miss how we are our own oppressors.

Honor yourself precisely because you are different. The configuration of your identity changes from day to day. Emptiness means your identity is not fixed or separate, always changing, always interdependent.

I suggest "suchness" is a more positive view of emptiness. The dynamic expression of the reality you are, its suchness, is a configuration arising out of many contingencies or changing variables. Lately, academics use the term "intersectionality." It seems similar. Intersectionality is the theory that identity categories are not mutually exclusive but integrated as a single multidimensional experience.

Race, gender, sexuality, physical traits, religion, education, family systems, etc. intersect to either increase or reduce discrimination. A pause to let this sink in could be useful. How many "identity categories" can you list for yourself?

In her *Wonderland* adventure, Alice remarked "I knew who I was this morning, but I've changed my mind a few times since then." Where do your changing identities overlap? Do you rank some above or below others? Can you describe a specific experience where you actually felt your ever-changing multidimensionality? For example, the gym could create the intersection of a physical trait, race, and age identities which are not the focus elsewhere. Are you vulnerable to dishonoring yourself by ignoring or even amplifying affliction in the tender spots where intersections shift and overlap? Here in the tender spots, where we so often hide in the shame of rejection, is the Wisdom jewel of suchness glowing as compassion.

Finally, honor your willingness to work with these teachings. Be patient but also persevere. Recently, a student who has been studying the new cosmology and practicing several years had what she called a "boing" moment. She had heard about the Great

Turning often but the words never really surged through her soul. In a note she described how they suddenly came alive. She "vibrantly realized turning toward one's true self and seeing the Larger Way."

This "boing effect" is often true for committed practitioners. A teaching we once heard is always working deeply within us. An "Aha!" will arise as a jewel of insight if we persevere. If we do not disparage ourselves. No matter how many times we may struggle to understand the teachings or try to do a practice may we offer ourselves "beginner's mind." Shunryu Suzuki is famous for saying, "In the beginner's mind there are many possibilities. In the expert's mind, there are few." (4)

Buddhists identify five hinderances to practice realization: *aversion, apathy, skeptical doubt, anxiety, and attachment.* We experience them according to our own conditioning. Consider the hindrance *aversion.* Some of us experience aversion most often toward others. Some of us turn aversion against ourselves. There are many variations for each hindrance. Once again, honor yourself. Accept and explore these hindrances as the many gateways to the Buddha Way. And then commit to ongoing study of the self. Only you can be alive as you.

THE SECOND ENCOURAGEMENT: ALLOW AWE

Welcoming awe is a way of welcoming yourself because, well, you are awesome! Each of us is already and always the shining suchness of infinite, radiant light. The phrase "This is awesome!" spoken in offhand ways used to annoy me: "That café's latest sandwich—*awesome!*" But with brief contemplative inquiry, the radiance of that sandwich can be disclosed. Where did the grain for the bread come from? What about the tomato and the onion? And then there's the creativity of the cook, the labor of the farmers, and the suppliers who brought the ingredients.

What is the source of all this energy? Trace it back and you will find the oxygen these humans needed and received from the trees. You will find the fertile soil, the waters and sunshine in everything on your plate. Existence is awesome inter-being.

"We are feeding on starlight!" said a scientist on *NOVA*. Track down the PBS *NOVA* series *The Universe Revealed* for many awesome insights and images.

The original radiant energy of the entire cosmos is expressing itself as the suchness of all these forms. In you with each delicious bite you swallow. In the darkness of your inner organs, that grain, that tomato, and all that labor are giving themselves to be metabolized as your energy. Now the sandwich is your opportunity. How will you express original radiance? You are endless possibility. In *The Light that Shines Through Infinity: Zen and the Energy of Life* (5) Dainin Katagiri, Roshi writes:

> *Light is the original nature of your life. Everyone has that light. It is the core of your personality that Buddhism is always talking about. But it's very difficult to know what it is because light is nothing but energy, motion, or dynamic functioning; your conscious mind can never pick up anything in particular. If you try to conceptualize it, your original nature is dark and dim for you because you can't see it in that way.*
>
> *Still, even though it cannot be conceptualized, it can be displayed because light is always functioning in your life. You can give play to it in every aspect of your life. So if you see something wonderful, don't get stuck! Accept it, experience it.... Your experience will never disappear. It stays with your life and penetrates your life. It's not necessary to attach to it. Let it go! (42-43)*

We don't need blissful visions or a trip to the Grand Canyon to experience awe. Mystics of all traditions have been awed by little things—a hazelnut (Julian of Norwich), a grain of sand (William Blake), a mustard seed (both Jesus and Zen monks). Rumi mentions that many people realize that the single drop of water is one with the whole ocean, and like Dogen's *Genjo Koan*, Rumi also adds that the entire ocean is actually contained in the single drop. Your small single drop of existence contains totality. Rumi echoes Katagiri: "You are the whole works."

Allowing awe grows from a commitment to mindfulness. Beginning with basic mindfulness of nonjudgmental, attentive presence we can go deeper. Four mindful soul movements—wonder, silence, reverence, and love—can be practiced.

Hold one palm open in your other hand. With the soft eyes of a meditative gaze, be present without thinking. Simply be in wonderment with your hand. Then exhale, relax into deeper silent presence. Allow a sense of mystery. Let your hand receive your reverence; it is a unique miracle. Such intimacy with your hand may naturally open your heart in love. (6)

Moving mindfully from wonder, silence, reverence into love cultivates awe and also gratitude. We begin to pause more often in the presence of a sunflower, the touch of a breeze. But we do not exclude the awe offered in unpleasant experiences. The smell of a decaying animal's corpse and the sound of the buzzing flies, the sight of plastic debris in a river—everything is the awe-full suchness of reality.

A few decades ago, I began studying the new cosmology taught by some contemporary scientists who honor the oneness of science and the sacred. Indigenous peoples have always lived within a sacred Universe but most Westerners have been conditioned by many centuries of splitting divinity and matter. One of these non-dualistic scientists is Brian Swimme. Swimme is a mathematical physicist who studied with cultural historian Thomas Berry. Berry was deeply influenced by Teillard de Chardin's vision of a sacred evolving Universe. Swimme embodies the union of the scientist and the mystic. Swimme's engaging videos, podcasts, lectures, and books, available online, have awakened awe in many non-scientists. I encourage you to experience his enthusiasm for our conscious evolution. (7)

This handbook began as an invitation to participate in the Great Turning. But can one person live as the Universe aware of Itself? Here's an example. John Seed, a rainforest activist in Australia, was ready to give into despair in the 1980s. But he was turned around from his personal despair when he had a major realization: he suddenly saw that *he* was the rainforest protecting itself! He turned his work into what is now known as "deep ecology." He and Joanna Macy have partnered to offer deep ecology rituals such as "The Council of All Beings" to help others embody their evolving consciousness of inter-being. (8)

In my view, these contemporary activists, scientists, mystics, and teachers offer insight into the vision of the Mahayana, an evolutionary turn in the Buddha Way: seeing the physical cosmos as the body of Buddha. A specific Buddha, *Vairocana*, is considered a personification of the awakened body of an aware Universe. Where is Vairocana manifesting now? How is awakened reality actually aware?

I think the evidence is in the acts of the human persons who make Great Turning choices. They have inspiration in the Bodhisattva Samantabhadra, who vows to actualize Vairocana's awakened body. Samantabhadra's name means "Universal Good." But where is Universal Good to be discovered these days? Only as a fantasy of a future utopia? No.

Universal Good cannot be made or destroyed by us. It is not a place. It was never "made." Primordial Goodness Just Is. We manifest Universal Good by liberating buddha nature. Universal suffering is the restraining force of deluded perception. Personal practice realization is transforming delusion into Wisdom's luminous Light. Take to heart this paraphrase of a famous proclamation by the early Christian Iraneus: "The Glory of the

Universe is YOU fully alive." Your full aliveness is conscious evolution. You are the Great Turning. There is no doubt—you are awesome.

THE THIRD ENCOURAGEMENT: YOU ARE NOT ALONE

Inter-dependent co-arising or "inter-being," means that all the buddhas (fully enlightened beings) and bodhisattvas (beings continuously enlightening other beings) support you in practice realization. Multitudes "as immeasurable as the sands of the Ganges" are exerting their strength for you, Dogen proclaims in *Jijuyu Zammai*.

As you aspire to awaken for all beings, all buddhas and bodhisattvas rejoice. As you study and forget the self, they are ready to be invoked. As you wait in the dark of unknowing, their radiance is shining. And as you step out in the spring dawn to actualize your freedom, all buddhas "increase the Dharma-joy of their original source." (*Jijuyu Zammai*)

When the historical Buddha fulfilled his awakening at dawn under the morning star, sitting at the foot of a fig tree, his proclamation included you: "I, along with all beings, am awakened."

Dogen gets quite specific about the subtle mutual assistance provided for us. *Jijuyu Zammai* is the self-receiving and giving of practice realization going on reciprocally. In *Jijuyu Zammai*, we read:

> *The trees and grasses and the land involved in this all emit a bright and shining light and preach the profound and incomprehensible Dharma...for the sake of ordinary people, sages and all living beings.*

And in turn, we "preach and exalt the Dharma for the sake of trees, grasses, walls and fences." Consider the current climate catastrophes. Aren't the rising seas, the extreme heat waves, vanishing habitats, the bleached coral reefs proclaiming the

Dharma to us loud and clear: "Wake up!" The cries of the Earth Body are now so evident that more and more humans are coming together to turn around the trajectory currently headed toward the massive loss of planetary life. Will we accept the challenge to turn toward practice and allow ourselves to be turned by the Love that makes the world go 'round. "Love makes the world go 'round"—a small, sweet Hallmark greeting actually proclaiming a very Big Thing.

It is important to recognize and receive subtle mutual assistance through sharing our grief, anger, and despair for the world. We are personally experiencing and/or witnessing the cruelty of humans toward each other and our Earth companions. Collective suffering is one body. Basic structures of human society are collapsing. Take considerable care. In protecting ourselves, we protect others.

You are not alone if you feel a tension in how to balance your contemplative inner life with outer action. I've seen the old slogan, "Don't just sit there, do something!" rephrased on tee shirts as, "Don't just do something, sit there!" Do you sense how both slogans need not be in opposition?

Your authentic doing flows through our shared being. They inter-are. Consider these words of renowned poet Lucille Clifton:

> *"In the bigger scheme of things, the Universe is not asking us to do something. The Universe is asking us to be something. And that's a whole different thing."*

Here, Tracy K. Smith, another great U.S. poet, also African American, is quoting Clifton for a *New York Times* book review. Smith ponders whether our thriving as a species hinges on asserting not to a different manner of doing, but of being. (9)

An ancient mantra from Taoist Wisdom is "The way to do is to be." Another formulation is "stillness in action." Dogen's teachings combine the active turnings of the outer circle and the fundamental still point of the eternal present.

Your inter-being is a profound synergy. Dogen says, "All things are intimately and imperceptibly assisting each other." Recall a surprising "Aha!" moment in your life. Was there a sense of receiving something mysterious and also feeling changed? You might also have sensed a call to live as that change. Such synergy is mostly unnoticed by human consciousness but inter-being pervades existence.

I received a lovely teaching that may help you if you feel alone and helpless. My Udumbara dharma sister, Tricia Teater, taught it to me and I've shared it often with my students: "Stop, watch … Listen … Listen. Remove the 'I' and you'll know what to do."

So pause before you ask whether you are doing enough for the world. Listen for the deeper Wisdom arising from your essence, where doings arise from your true being. As such, we are all "essential" workers.

DISCOVERING HOW YOUR CIRCLE SHOWS UP

"The most radical thing any of us can do at this time is to be fully present to what is happening in the world," says Joanna Macy. (10) Each world happening is a dharma door for entering your circle. Many buddhas are entering with you.

The ancient teachings predict that after the historical Buddha, Gautama Shakyamuni, the next Buddha for our planet will be named *Maitreya*. This Buddha will probably be a community, not an individual, according to many teachers, including Thich Nhat Hanh. We are most profoundly not alone when we reconfigure the self as global. A richer experience of the world-wide community also includes beings of deep time—past and future, as well as present.

Here's a story of envisioning future buddhas from Joanna Macy's life. A bodhisattva in her nineties, Macy has used her Buddhist training and her expertise in systems theory to share a life of practice realization. Her vision of the Great Turning as a spiral is quite similar to Dogen's Circle. You will find an explanation and some of her practice realization activities on her website, www.joannamacy.com, and her teachings through *The Work that Reconnects*. Also, see her book (with Chris Johnson) *Active Hope: How to Face the Mess We're in without Going Crazy*. (11)

In 1980, she was doing field work with the Sarodaya movement in Sri Lanka. This movement is dedicated to the work known as "Everybody Wakes Up." Macy led nonviolent direct-action workshops during the pre-civil war polarization of the Sinhalese and Tamil populations. One day in her room in the Quaker Center, Joanna had a visionary experience of Prajna Paramita, the Mother of all Buddhas, which revealed how the community there was in the birth labor of "Buddhas-to-be." She writes:

> *In that moment my life fell open and the Mother of all Buddhas wove herself into the fabric of my being...Since then, when I face a room full of strangers and feel at a loss, she shows up as soon as I invite her, holding me in her presence. Each time I need her, I find her anew--fresh, luminous and empty of preconceptions...I experience our mutual belonging in this beautiful suffering world and know there is ultimately nothing to fear. (12)*

My circle of the way has shown up through Joanna Macy's work and writings. I've been privileged to train with Joanna two times in my life. I've experienced how she midwifes "Maitreya" buddhas for the future. In 1980, I lived in Cheyenne near Warren Air Force Base with a Catholic Worker Community. Wyoming Senator Dick Cheney wanted to deploy the MX missile at that base. The MX was an offensive weapon targeting Russian cities.

Joanna was offering a "Despair and Empowerment" training in Boulder, Colorado, in conjunction with protests at the Rocky Flats Defense Department's plutonium production site. When I signed up to participate in "Despair and Empowerment" training, I was in a dark night of the soul, but not only because nuclear war might be imminent. I was personally burnt out from activist work in Cheyenne and at the Pentagon.

Our group, "Wyoming Against the MX," was obstructed by military and political forces. Phones were tapped. The local bishop did not want a religious woman "making trouble." I got a letter from him saying that he discontinued the social action teams I had formed in local parishes. My soul felt shredded.

Long ago, I found a saying that described this pain: "If doing is first, being vanishes. If being is primary, doing is empowered." Years of striving relentlessly to be "holy" by *doing* more and more did me in—an apt phrase. But to be "done" with that doer "me" was paralyzing. I was in despair when the workshop began. Joanna's midwifery practices with me then and with so many others worldwide arose from her own dark night. She recalled it in early 2020:

> *...immobilized, as if turned to stone, my whole body deadened by the eclipse of a livable future. And yet the message came, 'Just fall in love with what is'--a clear call for acceptance.* (13)

Another "Despair and Empowerment" participant half a world away in Britain, Jane Reed, wrote that, "*...participating in the intensive turned my life on its axis with new experiences of power, purpose and comradeship that reframed everything.*" (14)

"Reframing everything" is a succinct practice realization skill. It's tough. First of all, we have to see the framing process of the self. Neuroscience demonstrates how quickly the habitual frame gets set up. Then we allow the frame of "me" to dissolve.

Enlightenment is the restructuring of the whole self to realize the frameless eternal Self.

Thirty years later, in the summer of 2012, our local "Work That Reconnects" group brought Joanna—then in her 80s—to Madison, Wisconsin. What a celebratory full circle to practice with her again in a community of Buddhas-to-be of diverse religions, ages, colors, and gifts. Joanna says her life is an experience of "the sheer size of the human heart—so big I could walk into it. (15)

Your circle is a choice always on offer. When we feel alone, it helps to renew our trust in the omnipresent Universal Heart being shaped by our personal hearts.

Feel your own heart beat. Invite it to beat in synchronicity with the hearts of all those alive now. With each exhale, you can release your grip on fear. Sophia Zen student Julia encouraged our sangha: "Relax...let the ego drop into its proper place." Free fall into radical love with everything and everyone. You'll know what to do.

If you hear a voice saying, "Your actions are trivial; you're not doing enough," stop that voice. You may need to shout! Practice the "who" question. Investigate—"who" holds the gavel pronouncing judgement on your life? What force in your conditioning has such power over your true heart's intention? Skeptical doubt is the hindrance that questions and subverts your capacity to awaken. Great Doubt challenges skeptical doubt. It is the seeing power that shines Wisdom's light through these obstructions. Where else will energy for making evolution's Great Turning arise, if not in each human heart. Your personal circling is interconnected energy. No one suffers alone. No one is liberated alone.

Living the teachings of practice realization in a confusing world of immense anguish can feel overwhelming and impossible. I remember a great line from *Alice in Wonderland*. When

Alice heard her task commanded by the White Queen, she cried "That's impossible!" The Queen tut-tutted, "My dear, why sometimes, I've believed as many as six impossible things before breakfast."

The Bodhisattva vow to save all beings and end all delusion is impossible from the ego's perspective. Such a vow is grounded in great trust in the path of awakening. It is why we take refuge— in our buddha nature, in the teachings, and in each other. Trust that you are already where the path can take you is not slacking off but persevering. It is in the specific daily commitment to sit zazen and to study the way as we live into the teachings that original enlightenment is cultivated.

Cultivation is like training. Gifted musicians and professional athletes keep training. They usually consult with colleagues and with their coaches and teachers. I check in with Diane and other teachers often. Many of the specific ways to work with the teachings in this handbook are from my students. Boundless bows of gratitude to each of them! The practices can be helpful to individuals but are best used in the context of sangha support. If you do not have a sangha, spiritual community, or a teacher, ask yourself, "Why?" What holds you back from the gift and challenges of such support? Explore your conditioning and how hindrances, such as apathy and anxiety, can take over. Discover new capacities beyond current perspectives. Keep going courageously. Always seek professional help if you need it.

It is important to recognize that "growing up" into our full humanity needs to be cared for simultaneously with the process of "waking up."

The verbs you just read—explore, discover, keep going, seek help, be integrated—make a daunting list. There is a danger in splitting your aspiration from where you are now. Dogen's teaching that your practice now *is* realization is radical. You are not training to become something you are not. In fact, I consider

Zen training to be more like "entraining." Baby birds and some mammals "entrain." The word means "to draw oneself along" in the way the baby animal bonds with the mother or a substitute. Your buddha nature is already drawing you along. You are being "entrained" to awaken.

The work can be interior or exterior, "on the cushion or off the cushion" as the saying goes, Whether you are part of a social action project or experiencing your life in a hospice bed, begin with your intention. The "how" of doing anything can enact the ethical imperative inherent in practice realization. When I get discouraged about not doing "enough," it helps to recall this turning phrase of Diane's: *"As I continuously liberate my own suffering, I help others automatically."*

Your commitment to the circle of the way is already more than "enough." Each breath brings new energy. As Diane writes at the opening of Chapter Three, *"Today a new heart trail sparks a thousand ways to meet."*

The word "discover" implies that a covering has been discarded. We learn to "dis" the "cover" over our lives so that what was hidden is revealed." Your originally free buddha body is present no matter how your human body is caught in linear time. Practice realization is the commitment to see through obstructions that cover over the True Self. Discoveries are endless.

Can you recall the first stirring of a call to embark on a inner journey? Maybe now you can see how you've moved through many cycles of the circle of the way. There is regression but I now can quickly recognize who I've named (kindly) "old, fixed Paula." Her afflicted heart*mind is the precise place where Prajna Paramita's wise compassion offers me the choice of liberation. And it is a choice.

Wisdom wakes us up to how the ego is producing suffering—for ourselves or others—but we can often be stubborn. We stay put—like the panther in Rilke's poem. It takes Great Courage to choose freedom. Every time we do so, we are renewing our original intention. Through gradual maturation and refinement, instead of taking years or months of moving around the circle, we can turn through the circle in an hour or a few moments. "Somersaulting" or "cartwheeling" through the way, as Dogen liked to say.

SEVEN SUGGESTIONS FOR HONORING YOUR CIRCLE

Here are ways that allow the mystery of your soul's turnings to take form.

1) Perhaps using story form, making a scrapbook, a photo montage will help you discover how the phases of the circle have shown up in your past. By reflecting on your early years, you may detect early stirrings of the soul's yearning.

2) A good way to shift beyond linear time is to imagine your life as a fairy tale or mythic journey. "Once upon a time in a land far away..." provides a valuable larger and non-judgmental perspective. Recall your personal favorite fairy tale or hero from the myths. Do the abandoned children Hansel and Gretel or does Jack and his scary quest up the beanstalk feel familiar? Could Persephone, Icarus, or Innana offer a mirror for your life? Try rewriting these tales. Be the author telling your own mythic story.

3) If writing is not your most accessible skill, consider other modes to portray and honor the cycles of your life. Someone I know has done so with dolls and puppets she dressed in different costumes. Another created a series of archetypal masks to honor her soul's stories.

4) The classic archetypes—seeker, innocent child, warrior, victim, destroyer, wisdom figure, and more—are often revealed in your dreams. A dream journal or sketchbook is helpful. These archetypal patterns also

surface if we learn to see into our inner life being portrayed in the collective culture.

5) Perhaps there is a novel or a film that draws you back to relive over and over. What is it mirroring for you? Perhaps there are songs and lyrics that capture different phases of your life. From country music to jazz or folk songs, what is the "play list" of your life? How about inventing your own rap? Would your soul sing or dance to the blues or Debussy?

6) If you hesitate to draw or paint your inner life, let the art work of others serve as your mirror. I still have a worn-out print of *Judith with the Head of Holofernes* by Felice Fecerelli. It portrays Judith's heroic act of rescue for the Hebrew people. Early in my Zen training, I faced a showdown with my inner Holofernes. The painting mirrored the courage I needed to "behead" that internalized oppressor and silence its bullying voice.

7) If we are alert to images from diverse cultures and eras of human experiences, many mirrors will present themselves. For example, the self-portraits Frida Kahlo painted might also shine a light for you. Sometimes she paints her crippling injuries. Sometimes she portrays the tension of mixed ethnicities. She also honors herself as a dark and noble Earth Mother.

Whether it is work found in a museum or a mural painted on a city street, art can help us see and feel more widely and deeply into and beyond a personal joy or sorrow. Artworks are windows into the shared human soul.

While each of us ensouls the archetypal energies of the collective psyche, it takes commitment to grow ever more conscious of this process. Making the darkness conscious is the work of wholeness. Whether you use memoir, myth, music, visual imagery or other modalities, you can discover a way into the dark, unknown life that needs to be lived. Practice realization activities keep us attentive to our discoveries. The creative powers of the Universe are waiting under the surface to reveal the treasure of your true vastness. As Dogen says, you are being "actualized by myriad things." (*Genjo Koan*)

Some skeptics may demean this work of discovery as "navel gazing." That term is strangely appropriate. In Zen, self-discovery work is not private and anything but "navel gazing." Remember the earlier section on the alaya, the universal womb/storehouse. You are discovering the umbilical-cord connection to interrelated wholeness.

When you move into your soul's unknown life, you are also moving within the soul of the world. Some early Western philosophers called the world soul the "*anima mundi*." They associated the world soul with the divine Wisdom, waiting to become conscious in us. Sophia (Prajna Paramita) pours forth *from* the future.

In the twentieth century, the philosophy of the world soul was reframed by Carl Jung. He agreed that the world has a shared interior life and named it our collective unconscious. The alaya, the world soul, the Jungian container of all the world's unconscious—all describe the potential of humanity's awakenings of goodness and love, as well as all the residue of all our greeds and hates, fears, and traumas.

Obviously the collective soul of humanity has not yet been transformed. We keep producing suffering, generation after generation. Your personal suffering is a participation in *the* suffering of the world soul. It takes training to change from the experience of grief as *my* grief to realizing it is also *the* grief of everyone.

Wisdom is waiting for us to midwife the future. One by one, as each of us births our buddha nature and lives it, the collective womb stirs. Universal primordial Good awakes, conscious of Itself through us.

Apply this teaching to a specific experience.

Wisdom's seeing power will show you how you how are clinging to suffering personally. Perhaps you are hanging onto anger because the boss was rude to you. If you choose to let go of the anger, your release is now free energy. You've helped midwife a future of liberation, one with Universal Good.

This is Dogen's promise in *Jijuyu Zammai*: "...when even one person at one time sits in zazen, they become imperceptibly one with each of the myriad things and permeate completely all time."

Hear Dr. Martin Luther King Jr.'s famous proclamation as directed to you: *you* are turning the long arc of the moral universe toward justice.

Choosing to release your small anger really is a big deal. This is the bodhisattva vow to save all beings in its most intimate sense. These ancient teachings are especially urgent in our time when the collective soul of humanity is exploding in violence, surging with fear, and enduring cataclysmic sufferings. In the "ICU" of "Earth Emergency," there may not be many future generations sharing a viable planet able to do this work.

Universal awakening is not a distant dream. It is happening— or not—through each of us. Discovering how the circle of the way shows up in your life is the beginning step. Next is the choice to enter.

Notes to Chapter Four

(1) This is the translation given by Kosho Uchiyama in *Dogen's Genjo Koan: Three Commentaries*, Counterpoint, Berkeley, 2011, p150.

(2) Harper and Row, New York, 1989.

(3) Genesis 9:1, *The Bible in Today's English Version*. American Bible Society, New York, 1976.

(4) *Zen Mind, Beginner's Mind: Informal Talks on Zen Meditation*, Weatherhill, New York, 1970, p21.

(5) Edited by Andrea Martin, Shambhala Publications, Boulder, 2007.

(6) I learned this practice from Robert Sardello during an interfaith retreat on Sophia some years ago.

(7) See for example the excellent interview with Swimme entitled, "Comprehensive Compassion" by Susan Bridle in *What is Enlightenment?* magazine, Issue 19, Spring-Summer 2001. Swimme explains haw the physical cosmos is no different from spiritual reality. He calls us to "reinvent ourselves, at the species level" … around the whole Earth community. "That's the ultimate sacred domain." (Available online.)

(8) Discover this and more in *A Wild Love for the World: Joanna Macy and the Work of Our Time*. Edited by Stephanie Kaza, Shambhala Publications, Boulder, 2020, p49-62.

(9) *New York Times Book Review*, Oct. 3, 2021, 1, p20.

(10) *A Wild Love for the World*, p30.

(11) New World Library, Navoto, CA, 2012 and on "The Work That Reconnects" website.

(12) *A Wild Love for the World*, pp301-304.

(13) Ibid., p77.

(14) Ibid., p41.

(15) Ibid., p358.

ENTRY POINTS AND SKILLFUL MEANS

INTRODUCTION– EXPLORING YOUR POSITION IN THE CIRCLE

The author Arundhati Roy describes each moment as a "portal," an entry point between one world and the next. Roy's image was invoked by Ojibwe tribal member and social activist Winona La Duke as she spoke of protecting tribal lands and waters at the Enbridge pipeline expansion. La Duke saw standing at "Line Three" as a portal. She challenged us with her question "What do you want to bring through the portal?" (1)

Dogen's term for this portal is the central pivot. We have a choice to enter the portal with two types of energy—backsliding into our old habits and fears or letting go of predictable patterns and walking through freely, open handed. We can, and do, miss the moment of choice. When we are numb or on "auto-pilot," for example.

Portals for stepping through a moment open-handed and into practice realization are everywhere, especially within our body and our senses. Sensation is attentive in any type of experience— especially ones outside our comfort zone where it is easy to shut down. Entry points are especially startling in graces of "Aha" moments. The obstructing patterns of the small self can fall away in an instant. We can be turned into a brief awakening, *kensho,* as Wisdom's light breaks through. The deep heart*mind is always ready to open. It is easy to miss our opportunities.

Generally we don't pause for long but keep moving on to the next thing that grabs our attention—a different sensation or a new thought. If our intention to awaken is strong, we will learn to pause. We practice staying present so we may realize the "Aha" as a portal into mystery, even when it shows up as the "Oh No!" of a shock.

Did you learn a maxim for fire drills in grade school? I was taught this one: STOP, DROP, and ROLL. When your clothing catches on fire, you must not run but "STOP, then "DROP"—lie on the floor—and finally "ROLL"—turn over to smother the flames. This simple maxim is a skillful means to fully enter any experience.

A Sophia Zen Sangha member told us of picking raspberries in a community garden. A beetle was gnawing away at a young plant. Then she saw many of the plants were infested. At first, she recoiled in disgust. This was the "clothes on fire" moment. But she did not "feed the flames," so to speak. She stopped the reactive energy of aversion toward the beetle. She dropped into mindful presence. Her "roll" was turning the reaction of disgust around. The "drop" of letting it go allowed kindness to arise naturally from her heart*mind. She told us she felt the beetle's need to survive was the same as her own. This experience lasted only a few seconds but it seems to me that she made a full turning into and through Dogen's circle. Because she is a committed practitioner, she was not mindlessly picking raspberries. So when the beetle appeared, she paused long enough to recognize an entry point for practice to realize an appropriate response.

I think our most available entry point for practice realization is one we often miss. Whether we acknowledge it or not, we are of this Earth and its elemental powers of air, fire, water, and land. Its changing seasons, the weather and the billions of species here with us are offering us entry points. If we are paying attention, we will be present when they momentarily intersect with our personal experience.

Perhaps you are familiar with poet Mary Oliver. Most of her poems offer precise, sensitive descriptions of entry points into awakening: a specific grasshopper, a storm, just lying on the grass. Oliver and other poets such as Rumi and Rilke offer many portals into our universal religious impulse. The multi-cultural collection in *Poetry of Presence: An Anthology of Mindfulness Poems* is a treasure. (2)

Early *homo sapiens* responded to the powers of nature with awe and fear. The human dependence on nature for survival was starkly evident. After the Neolithic revolution, most humans prioritized the rational mind for technological solutions that would make us less vulnerable to nature. Many inventions have been useful. However, any new technology can and has been used to reinforce hierarchical dualisms. Perhaps the worst moments of climate catastrophes can be portals to healing and compassion if we learn to turn again first to nature as did our early ancestors.

The renowned cultural historian, scholar of world religions, and Catholic priest Thomas Berry called us to this "Great Work." As the last century ended, Berry wrote:

> *The Great Work before us, the task of moving modern industrial civilization from its present devasting influence on the Earth to a more benign mode of human presence, is not a role we have chosen...But even as we make our transition into this new century, we must note that moments of grace are transient moments. The transformation must take place within a brief period. Otherwise it is gone forever. In the immense story of the*

97

universe, that so many of these dangerous moments have been navigated successfully is some indication that the universe is for us rather than against us...It is difficult to believe that the purposes of the universe, of the planet Earth, will ultimately be thwarted, although the human challenge to these purposes must never be underestimated. (3)

Visionary elders and courageous young people such as Greta Thunberg inspire us to live in humble communion as an Earth community. While world religions provide many symbols and stories from nature as teachings, it is important to directly enter into the natural world as yourself. Meet the grasshopper or the thunderstorm yourself.

For example, how does the dark of winter feel to you? Is it an invitation to stillness, a time of loss, or something else? Receive the teachings of the seasons, of rocks and shorelines, of burning embers and misty rain as they reveal themselves to you. They are dharma doors. The Dharma is the Way the Universe is teaching in Katagiri Roshi's definition (see page 27). Dogen connects the four seasons and four times of day with his experiences of practice realization. Your symbols and metaphors for the circle may be different.

Animals have always helped humans enter spiritual realms, most especially within indigenous cultures. Out of respect for the unique relationship of an indigenous people with the animals, lands, waters, and plants, who are their sisters and brothers, non-native persons are cautioned not to appropriate indigenous ways. For example, if the wolf seems to be a powerful teacher for you, do your own inner work to discover what this animal is specifically asking of you. Don't mimic or misuse another's entry point. Animals carry soul energy for many of us perhaps because their consciousness is so similar to ours. Yet it appears animals are not caught in the dualistic thoughts born of human language.

I've often wondered about their experience of what we name buddha nature.

Recently, I came across a book by David Hinton, a beautiful reflection on Chan poetry. He quotes a line from Tu Fu as the poet encounters some deer:

> *[I] face deer at my bramble gate: so close here, we touch our own kind in each other.*

Hinton comments that the deer "are sage indeed.... They are always already awakened. Because they are free of our reflexive self-identity, that mirrored opening is the nature of their everyday experience. And also, because they exist without the naming that divides reality into its 10,000 forms, they inhabit reality as a single existence tissue." (4)

Tu Fu's experience with the deer is his entry point. Poetry is his skillful means. What animal, fish, or insect, what plant, mountain, river, or desert is your entrance into this deeper life?

Living that question over and over during your day in any situation is what Zen calls knowing one's "dharma position." Dharmas—with a small "d"—are all the ordinary phenomena showing up, changing, disappearing, and "positioning" themselves for a time in personal experience. The myriad dharmas co-mingling with you offer the opportunity to drop into the wider and fuller self. All that is required is your mindful attention.

In *The Extensive Record*, (Vol. 10, #21), Dogen describes being wholeheartedly present in our lives:

> *Every bit of your sincere heart pervades the heavens...but unless you clarify many times with your whole body, after one doubt comes another.*

In other words, be mindful during the day. Stop and pause often. Drop deep to confirm your intention and not subvert your awakening with distraction or doubt. Enter the mystery of your aliveness skillfully and consistently. This request sounds lovely, yes, but it is not easy to be fully alive. Consider this quote I've kept for many years: *"Everyone is dealing with how much of their own aliveness they can bear and how much they need to anesthetize themselves."* (Adam Philips). It takes great courage to be a mindful human being.

Here's a message from Diane to conclude this section. She printed it in large script and posted in Udumbara Zen Center. Before you read it, please look around the space you are in right now. Let your attention settle gently upon something specific nearby.... Here are the words: *"Something so profound entering, that needs holding, that could easily be passed on by."*

YOUR BASIC FOUNDATION: MINDFULNESS AND ZAZEN

The next four sections offer an array of choices for discovering your dharma position, entering the experience, and using skillful means for going deeper. Some options are pretty involved but they all begin with a basic foundation: ongoing mindfulness and daily zazen.

There are many descriptions of mindfulness these days. For a fine discussion of the authentic Buddhist tradition, I recommend the chapter on Right Mindfulness in the text, *The Eightfold Path*, cited earlier. Take note in the popular media of ways mindfulness practice can be been co-opted to pursue the goals of ego or corporate success. Authentic mindfulness as taught in Buddhist texts is not attached to the "gaining mind."

The basic form is sustaining an attentive, non-judgmental presence with whatever is arising in your experience. There is a simple way to bring mindful presence into your day. Remember to take three breaths. When you are shifting from one activity, stop to pause for three inhalations, three exhalations. Such wholehearted mindfulness in this moment will support you as you move into whatever is next.

One woman in Sophia Zen Sangha is a chaplain at a Madison hospital. She practices mindfulness as she approaches the door of each patient's room. With her hand on the door, she stops to breathe mindfully. Then she opens the door, ready to greet the patient.

Stillness with mindful breathing—so simple. Because we so frequently pass by the chance to intentionally enter our lives, the first breath stops us from auto-pilot momentum. The second breath drops us deeper. Here is the chance to let go and open fully so we are present for what will show up. After the third breath, we can move more mindfully into the new experience.

In addition to ongoing mindfulness, daily zazen is the foundation for practice realization. At least a half hour is encouraged. There are variations of course. In *The Eightfold Path*'s chapter on "Right Samadhi or Concentration," you will find a detailed description of how to practice zazen (157-159.) The website for the San Francisco Zen Center includes help for "Entering Practice" under its website offerings. The St. Paul MN Zen Center Clouds In Water site includes a video description of how to begin a practice.

Along with sitting zazen, some practitioners also do *kinhin,* or slow walking meditation. You can find many descriptions of how to sit formal zazen in ancient texts and from contemporary teachers. Take a look at a few websites for Zen centers for some examples. Dogen's instructions for traditional monastic zazen are in his essay *Fukanzazengi*, available online.

Zazen literally means "sitting (*za*) *zen*" So what does *zen* or *chan* in Chinese mean? A simple translation is "absorption." While in the posture of erect noble sitting, breathing naturally, we are wholeheartedly absorbed in alert, embodied attention. Attention to what?

Initially, we follow the breath as the object of our attention. We recognize and release any other object (such as a thought) and return to the breath. This is basic zazen. Sometimes the word *shikantaza* or "just sitting" is used. Here the object we attend to—the breath—is also released. There is no longer an object for a subject to observe. The word *shikan* is usually translated as "just" or "only." *Ta* can mean "precisely" and *za* is sitting. Shikantaza is "just precisely sitting."

Thoughts will come. Just sit without attaching and following thoughts; without pushing them away. Dogen calls this "non thinking." We don't try to stop thinking nor do we get involved in thinking. I recommend the excellent anthology, *The Art of Just Sitting: Essential Writings on the Zen Practice of Shikantaza*, for in-depth understandings. (5) Of course, the best way to discover the power of sitting is to just sit. The guidance of a teacher can support you.

The daily half-hour or forty minutes of sitting Soto teachers recommend is structured and formal. Informally, we continue the same wholehearted, alert, embodied presence in all our other "off the cushion" postures and activities—our ongoing, intentional, mindful life. Formal zazen provides a focused time to study the self by observing ways habitual thinking patterns show up and then releasing or "forgetting" them.

Sometimes, rejected dimensions of the psyche will show up during zazen so it is important to have access to a therapist if you need support.

Besides studying and forgetting the self in formal sitting, we also include ongoing contemplative inquiry. The examples below are ways of practicing contemplative inquiry. Your basic foundation and contemplative inquiry will open portals for stepping into practice realization each day.

WAYS TO WORK WITH THE TURNING PHRASES

If you skimmed through the turning phrases of Dogen's at the end of Chapter Two and Diane's in Chapter Three, now is the opportunity to go deeper. Before you choose a phrase, try asking "What is my dharma position now?" Then "just sit" for a bit to let current thought patterns, body sensations, moods, and emotional states show up.

How are you perceiving your relationships, social concerns, global issues? Not only your interior experiences but also wider realms of your life are shaped by how you are perceiving what is showing up. As the saying goes, what you see is what you get.

Next, note that one of the four sections of the turning phrases may be most relevant to an entry point for going below the surface situation. For example:

- If your life is unfocused, restless, confused, consider choosing the turning phrases for *aspiration*.

- The second phase, *practice studying and forgetting the self*, opens varied opportunities for discernment and depth.

- If you are in a difficult, fearful place or recognize you are at a dead end, you may be entering a dark night of the soul. See if the phrases honoring *enlightenment within darkness* offer you courage.

- If you are moving into greater sense of freedom or through a significant transformation, the phrases for *actualizing nirvana* may offer insight into how to live this new self.

Sense where in the circle you are now. Find a turning phrase in the section that most mirrors your life's dharma position. Enter here.

After reading a phrase of Diane's or Dogen's, pause. Extend the pause by closing your eyes and dropping into silence. After a few breaths, open your eyes, slowly read the phrase again. Notice what feelings, memories, or associations bubble up. Listen to the phrase move through your body. Grasping for a meaning splits you from direct experience. It starts producing a self that comments, names, analyzes, judges. Let go of that need to know and simply receive.

The process of working with the phrases is much like zazen. When you notice your mind has wandered away from the phrase, recognize that you've left it. Then release that distraction and return to silence. Wait and stay present. I call this the "3 R" process: **R**ecognize, **R**elease, **R**eturn.

There's a 4th "R" too: **R**elax. I've learned to trust the saying, "There's never a reason not to relax." Relax your facial muscles, eyes, jaw, and neck. So much energy gets crammed into the head. Release that thinking energy into the heart and the belly. Let it move through your body. Breathe with it, especially in the stillness of the exhale. Wait. You might find a few key words or that only one word that resonates. Let it be a mantra. Speak it out loud, whisper, chant, or make up a melody to sing it into memory. Writing it out on a slip of paper or a card can be helpful.

These skillful means honor the presence of the deeper mind within. All we need do is slow down and be still enough to allow the depths to surface. Sometimes you may experience synchronistic surprises. Seemingly out of nowhere, the phrase shows up. The great secret of your original wholeness is suddenly apparent. Dogen reminds us not to be fixated on getting a meaning. In *Jijuyu Zammai*, he teaches that our original enlightenment is working "inside and outside throughout the Universe. Yet such things are not mingled in (our) perceptions…" This hidden grace is what Dogen means by the "subtle mutual assistance" of all beings supporting your awakening. Out of nowhere, now here.

"THE READINESS IS ALL"

Before a race, the runners hear "Are you ready? Then they're told "Get set!" then finally "Go!" One way to apply Shakespeare's line, "The readiness is all," is to continually recommit to your original intention. The aspiration to wake up is an immense "ask" of yourself. You aspire to change the course of evolution! The turning phrases and other practices help us change the momentum of human existence—our own and everyone's—from the retrograde of ignorance into awakening wisdom for the future of human society. And the Earth.

On August 9th, 2021, the United Nations' panel on Climate Change announced that the planet is in "Code Red." Are you ready to stand in trust at this portal? Will you trust it as a transient moment of grace, as Thomas Berry says? All enlightening beings past, present, and future are in readiness to assist. The energy of the cosmos is available. Commenting on the "Black Lives Matter" movement, Robert Battle, artistic director of the Alvin Ailey Dance Theater, said: "It's not enough to reinvent the wheel—we need to roll it. (6)

In other words, don't reinvent your life based on a theory. Intellectual Zen is not enough. As Battle implies, revolutionary change needs to be the way you roll through life. Only you can turn the teachings into your life to actualize practice realization. In stillness, trust the pivot point. It is the meeting point of the relative—your gifts midst the world's needs—intersecting with Universal enlightening activity.

What if you feel stuck? Diane's phrases can be encouraging: *"An impasse can be good for the ego. What's the payoff for staying stuck?" "Are you willing to give up your current view of reality?"*

Like the "crawl" moving along the bottom of the TV screen, the same stories play through, then disappear from our thoughts. We know the cells in our bodies are being born and dying. Physics tells us every particle will collapse into a wave. During zazen, we learn to observe this flow of impermanence very intimately without attaching to a thought "particle."

But there are times when the freshness of beginner's mind seems impossible. Nothing shows up to offer an "Aha," a surprising or a shocking insight to stimulate our aliveness. The hindrance of apathy can pull us down into despair.

When I feel stuck, the words of Celtic poet John O'Donahue help me: *The work of love is always going on, beneath all other movement, at the bottom of the bottom.*

Here is an exercise that can help to loosen resistance. The intent is to discover keeps you from the readiness for transformation. I call it ...

"What Keeps You From...?"

- You will need a partner. The two of you sit face to face, ideally within a sangha or spiritual group. A leader or one of the participants has a bell and keeps time.

- Your partner reads to you from a card: *"Your name, what keeps you from moving into your full, true self?"* You give a brief answer, not a long speech. Just one word is also fine. Your partner says "Thank you."

- Your partner then repeats the same question. You give another brief answer. The partner says "Thank you." This exchange continues for several minutes until the leader rings a bell.

- Then you and your partner switch roles. When another bell is rung, you two change again. After a first round of switching, it is best to continue for more rounds.

- Moving to other partners in the group can be helpful. The leader senses when to close the exercise with the invitation to sit in silence or formal meditation.

I have found this exercise to be an effective way to soften hardened resistance. Cracking through tight layers of a self that does not trust its vastness or has little patience with gradual change can be tough. It can be like breaking through thick ice.

Have you heard of the skunk cabbage plant? I first found one along an iced-over stream in the Arboretum woods of the University of Wisconsin in Madison. It was early March. There was no sign of life visible anywhere. The nearby lake was locked in ice. Though the forest floor was covered in snow, deer and hikers had stomped a slushy trail. I made my way to a small bridge where I witnessed a strange phenomenon: a large, purply, bulbous plant had pushed its way through the ice. It was alive and thriving. There were other small ones poking up nearby.

Later, I learned the plant's name—skunk cabbage—because of its odor when the air warms up. To me, its capacity to generate its own inner heat, melt the ice, and then bust into bloom seems miraculous. My skunk cabbage pilgrimage is now a yearly event. It is a reminder that the work of blossoming is secretly going on "at the bottom of the bottom" even when we feel frozen in a dead end.

In her book, *The Pregnant Virgin*, Marion Woodman writes:

> *We plant our fat amaryllis bulb, we water it, put it in the sunlight, watch the first green shoot...and marvel at the great bell flowers tolling their alleluias to the snow outside. Why should we have more faith in an amaryllis bulb than in ourselves. It is because we know the amaryllis is living by some inner law—a law we have lost touch with ourselves.* (7)

The Law of the Universe, the Way it works, is one of the descriptions of the ultimate Dharma. The Universe's creative work is ordinarily hidden from our perception. When we feel stuck or experience hopelessness, we might want to give up on ourselves or our species. But the dead end of our personal view is precisely the place where profound transformation can begin. A breakthrough into wholeness cannot be willed by the ego. This is a painful place for the competent self that cries "What can I do?" It takes Great Courage to persist trusting *the work of love... always going on* whether we sense anything or not. Diane once posted an unpublished poem of Shunryu Suzuki Roshi's for us. I re-read it in such moments.

> *Don't move. Just die...over and over. / Don't anticipate. Nothing can save you now because you have only this moment./...With no future be true to yourself and express yourself fully./ Don't move.*

Here is another exercise for discovering how creative energy moves deep within. It is intended to destabilize the sense of a fixed self. Most of us have a handy "elevator speech" we use to sum up our identity. We might get thrown when our basic self-description is challenged. Many of the koans in Zen are paradoxical questions designed to challenge a surface response to the question "Who are you?

INSTRUCTIONS FOR THE EXERCISE "WHO ARE YOU?

- You and a partner sit face to face. One asks the question: "Who are you?" The partner responds briefly with no more than a simple declarative sentence, a phrase or just one word: "I am _____." This Q & A exchange repeats for 3 to 4 minutes.

- When the leader rings the bell, your roles switch. When the bell rings again roles switch again.

- This "Q & A" back and forth should continue as long as possible, at least a half hour. If the responder goes silent, the questioner waits for a while before again asking "Who are you?" Time for silence during and afterward is important.

My initial experience of this exercise continued for a full day as a group retreat led by a trained teacher. We took short breaks in silence and changed partners periodically. There was a time for a silent lunch and for walking meditation outdoors. Before the day concluded, we sat in meditation and had time for journaling about our experience. We then gathered in a circle so those who wished to share their practice could do so. The circle was not a group discussion. Individuals shared their struggles and discoveries of a deeper, wider, more fluid sense of self. Reverence grew for the mystery we each are. We ended by thanking our partners for their help.

I think this exercise can be offered in various formats—or done as a solo extended meditation with pen and paper—to fulfill the same intention: allowing the mystery of who you are to present itself in myriad ways.

Consider this analogy—it honors the courage the "Who Are You" exercise invites. Imagine a seascape where icebergs are floating about. In the first moments, the question "Who are you?" is easily answered by the mind at the tip of the iceberg, your conscious mind. Repeated questioning gradually stops ordinary thinking. New insights can open. Wisdom's light shines to melt layers of the surface self and to illuminate unknowns in the dark depths. This is the second phase of Dogen's circle: forgetting the self.

When Hamlet speaks "The readiness is all" in the play, he has finally come to believe that God's presence in every detail of life will be revealed at any moment: "If not now, yet it will come. The readiness is all." Your readiness to inquire again and again takes patience. But your persistence will be rewarded with understandings not available to ordinary surface consciousness.

Earlier, I mentioned a phrase in Chan ancestor Dongshan's *Song of the Jewel Mirror Awareness*: "Inquiry and response come up together." Inquiry is your turning practice. Response is being turned by a realization. A sincere, patient inquiry to your deepest questions will turn you into the illuminating response of Wisdom's jewel.

Maybe the response will not make sense or not appeal to the ego. Maybe the response will not be immediate. We do not control the type or timing of a response. But, when your soul is ready to step through the threshold of the known, offer your sincere unknowing to the Wisdom that is beyond your wisdom. Prajna Paramita is present, mirroring your deepest True Self. She has a clear knowledge of your own being for she does not stray away from it. (*Hymn to the Perfection of Wisdom*)

"DEEP CALLS TO DEEP"

"Deep Calls to Deep" is a phrase in Psalm 42 from the Hebrew Bible. This psalm is a cry for divine help made from a position of a soul willing to attune to the call of the unfathomable. There are many ways to deepen receptivity to Wisdom beyond your current understanding. Over time, ongoing inquiry to deeper practice will call forth further illuminating responses. We persevere even though the conscious mind can never fully comprehend the response. (8)

YOUR PRACTICE JOURNAL

I've emphasized the benefit of practice with a group, such as a sangha, with a teacher or guide, but ultimately this is *your* enlightenment process. How you wake up with all beings is yours uniquely, no one else's. It is easy to generalize about the path of awakening when we read spiritual books or listen to podcasts. But working with a journal is a way to experience your particular heart*mind's evolution. The practice journal can become your expression of circling through aspiration, practice, enlightenment, and nirvana.

We have already considered the skillful means of journaling in the context of working with the turning phrases. Now let's go deeper and wider. Some students rely on practice with a journal consistently. They are using the journal for help living Dogen's maxim: "To study the way is to study the self." (*Genjo Koan*) Others use their journal as needed. If a crisis erupts, a major question looms, or a shift is unfolding, the journal is a valued companion. Some journal only when their teacher asks them to do so. Usually this is because writing is not a readily accessible skill. "I don't know what to write!" some students tell me. Because the small mind often tries to ignore the Big Mind, I might ask them "What truth might be underneath your need to know what to write?"

It helps to explore our resistance. Why not use resistance as the topic to write about. Try asking, "Hey, blank journal, what do you want?" I love Diane's encouragement for staying with resistance: *Feel your gravity rocket of resistance drop away.*

If we make a sincere effort to investigate, Wisdom's depths will arise and will call to yours. Prajna Paramita, Sophia, is mothering your buddha nature. Her Wisdom is inviting your wisdom. I sense her whispering, "I will show you everything if only you persevere." If journaling becomes an impossible entry point, explore other modalities. Four Sophia Zen Sangha members describe their entry points in the Appendix.

A practice journal is the sutra of your life. *Sutra* in Sanskrit means thread. Our medical term "suture" comes from it. The many threads of the Buddha Way have been stitched together over the centuries, threading through various cultures. Now it is our turn.

The threads of your writings can become living expressions of how awakening is happening now. Some medical sutures are actually absorbed into the body once the stitching has assisted the body's natural healing. Likewise, your journaling's worded "stitches" are intended to disappear into the fibers of your life.

The words of the canonical Buddhist sutras are reverenced, yes, but they are not enshrined as fixed dogma. They are meant to be creatively lived into the future. In Essay #53, *Buddha Sutras* Dogen reflects on the significance of writing:

> *....future generations will be able to understand one-taste Zen based on words and letters if they devote their efforts to spiritual practice by seeing the universe through words and letters, and words and letters through the universe... what we mean by the sutras is the entire universe itself... words and letters are all regarded as the instruments of the great Way..."* (9)

The ordinary words and letters of journaling are your instruments for seeing the great Way of the Universe at work in your life.

A practice journal does not have to be grammatically correct, neat, or organized. In fact, such efforts can interfere with your inquiry and its response. Simply note the date. Pause to sink into silence. Make your sincere aspiration for awakening. Then just write. In each of the suggestions that follow, trust that your journaling is deepening and enlarging your soul. The soul is the bridge between the abstraction of ideas and the concrete physicality of your hand holding a pen moving across paper in this space at this time. Maybe some folks use a keyboard and a screen. What shows up in your journal reveals what your soul is discovering.

Here are a few ways to use a practice journal:

- **Journal before or after formal practice,** such as zazen, a Dharma talk, or an interview with your teacher. Free writing before formal practice can help to focus your intention and settle the so-called "monkey mind." Writing after the experience takes it more intimately within yourself. Perhaps something you heard in a talk or that arose during zazen needs to be opened into gratitude or explored with curiosity or compassion. Perhaps it needs to be held in a question for "don't know mind." Perhaps it starts connecting with memories, world events or. . .? Just write.

- **Journal to "pull over to the side of the road."** This is Diane's phrase for responding to a sudden arising. You probably won't have your journal handy when such a "pull-over-and-stop" event shows up to break through your typical momentum. Sometime later that day or the next morning, take the time to re-enter the experience. The intent is not to try to preserve it. That can reinforce the ego's view. Just sit with what showed up. Let what it wants to reveal or ask of you surface.

We especially need to "pull over" to stop the momentum of reactivity when affliction bursts into our lives. If you have had a close call while driving, perhaps you did stop and pull over to gather yourself together. Hearing a cruel swear words shouted at you or feeling the trigger of a painful memory can activate the suffering self. We can react in ways that make the situation worse. To continue the driving analogy, reactive road rage accelerates our suffering. But if we remember to stop and drop into the protection of our practice, even during a devastating experience, there can be space for three breaths. A non-reactive, mindful response to the situation is then more possible.

The purpose of journaling later is not to fix the event into memory. Instead the journal becomes the place to go below the surface narrative. Just as in zazen, it helps us attend to what arises from the deep mind without clinging.

Instead of taking everything personally, open beyond the small self's limited view. Hold the intention to connect the micro-threads of your experience within the macro-web of inter-being.

Journaling is a great way to "place yourself at the edge of your life," as Diane teaches. This is a key skill for liberation. It is a way to take what Dogen calls "the backward step." Just write.

- **Journal to discover how an experience, past or present, is constructed.** Diane taught us to make a diagram that visualizes how the self can be constructed or "set up" by past conditioning. Anything that is constructed can fall apart. A karmic affliction can deconstruct. Why? Because it is empty of permanence and independence. Try it.

1) In the center of a page, write a few words identifying an experience that is afflictive. For example, *"Why did I volunteer for this demanding project?"*

2)Then draw five lines extending toward the ego statement. Make the lines arrows pointing toward the center question.

3) On each line, write one of the 5 "Cs" to diagram the self's set-up. In the *Turning Phrases,* Diane gives a version of "5 Cs." Here are my labels for the diagram lines: *circumstances, my past conditioning, proximate cause, remote cause, and the broader context.*

4) Write what you recall about the situation for each line. Perhaps the *broad context* was, "The organization was losing staff." The diagram shows how you were "set up" by these "Cs" to make a choice that resulted

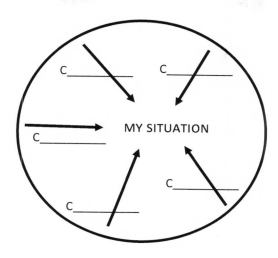

in suffering. It proves how that moment of "self-making" is constructed out of many "non-self" factors.

The possible *proximate* cause—a rushed meeting—and the *remote* cause—volunteering in the past—are not the self in this moment.

Here's the good news of impermanence! When you see how your afflictive self is an empty (i.e., a changing, interdependent construction), you can choose ways to let go of habits that set you up in the past. Diane's turning phrase applies: *"Giving up a fixed self is giving up something that isn't!"* What liberative skills might these be? Just write.

- **Journal to study sutras, chants, writings by Dogen and other teachings.** While studying, have your journal nearby. Here's an example for journaling with the well-known "Metta" or "Loving Kindness" chant. There are three rounds of requests. The first is for yourself. The second is for a neutral or troubling person. The third is for all beings.

The chant uses many versions of this format. To avoid vague generalities, get specific. For example: *"May I be free from suffering."* Pause to recognize a specific affliction you experience. This is followed by *"May you* (someone you care about)...." Pause to consider what this person is enduring. *"May X..."* Visualize the neutral or troubling person. How might they be suffering? Finally, *"May all beings..."* Visualize specific global situations of suffering.

When you offer the second round of requests, again pause to consider or imagine specific situations, persons, or events. *"May I receive loving kindness..."* continues for the subsequent persons (*"you," all beings."*).

The third request, *"May I live in peace"* is also offered for each. Use your practice journal to honor the unseen presence of each being for the three requests. Go deeper into each request. For example, actually describing an image of the troubling person receiving your loving kindness could be quite moving. Just write.

A text such as *The Heart Sutra* (see the Appendix) has been analyzed by many excellent scholars. Their work can serve you at the intellectual level. But journaling can invite the sutra to thread itself into your life.

Read slowly, pause. Let the sutra open line by line, phrase by phrase. Here are some specific skillful means:

> 1) **Stop when a word or image grabs you.** You might paraphrase these passages in your own words. Let insights or questions arise.

> 2) **You could address *The Heart Sutra* to yourself** (instead of Shariputra). For example, if you just received some upsetting news, it might help to see that its "form"—an email or a doctor's

call—is not your whole true self. Your news is not "yours" in isolation. It is interrelated with everything that is going on. This how compassion and emptiness work. You are saved from all suffering and distress when you let go. *The mind is no hindrance.*

3) **Rewrite the Sutra with a specific perspective**. I rewrote the Sutra at the onset of the Covid-19 pandemic. The rewrite helped me to realize that the virus is not a separate menacing "thing" but is inter-dependent with everything on Earth. The virus is actually a form within a universe of causes and conditions. When I "depend on Prajna Paramita," her wise compassion frees my mind of the hindrances (aversion, anxiety, apathy, etc.) that show up around the pandemic. Now the lines "without any hindrance no fears exist…" hold personal healing. Personalizing any classic text is not irreverent. Rather, you are inviting the ancient words to be new sutra of your life now.

I encourage you to use similes and metaphors in your writing and the other ways you express yourself. Find them when reading poetry or listening to song lyrics. Notice them in the writing of others. They are not irrelevant extras. Metaphors and similes are everywhere in spiritual writing. When people say, "God is my Rock," they are using a metaphor. Hildegard of Bingen wrote of her spiritual experience using a simile to express her particular spiritual experience: "My soul is like a feather on the breath of God." What about you? Ask the Deep Mind to offer you a metaphor for your spiritual life.

For example, Dogen says zazen can be like "groping for the elephant." That might or might not be true for you. For many years, whenever I sat alone, I struggled big time. I told Diane that zazen was like "drilling through granite." She got it immediately. She suggested that I relax and investigate why this was so.

Here's a sample metaphor/simile process to try for yourself. What is something you feel very uncertain about? "My uncertainty is a .... (*fill in the blank*). Let the inner feeling find an outer-world image that is authentic for you. Consider these two different images: My uncertainty feels like "waiting for a fireworks display." This image reveals a different truth than my uncertainty is like "waiting to lift the cloth over a corpse."

When you find yourself using a metaphor or simile or notice one written by someone else, stop to allow "deep call to deep." The Deep Mind will offer insight. What arises honors a particular experience as "Isness," awake and intimate.

We've ventured far beyond typical journaling in this section to include many creative ways of responding to unknown depths. What about the depths of sleep? Many people I know keep a dream journal. I use a separate small book beside the bed so it's in my reach as my eyes open.

As a Jungian analyst, Diane helps her students enter their dreams as dharma gates into the treasures of the unconscious. She once said, *"The dream channel is always 'on' Satori."*

Dogen explains this in Essay #39, *A Dream within a Dream.* He says the complete circle of the way is moving through our dreams:

> *In the dream state—equally in the waking state—there are arousing mind, training, enlightenment and nirvana. All phenomena in the dream state as well as the waking state are equally ultimate realities. Realization consists invariably of what a dream makes within a dream.*

We can learn to remember our dreams and record them. Being turned by realizations in dreamwork is a richly rewarding process worth investigating. The Jungian understandings of dreams are a place to begin.

There are many books about journaling as a spiritual practice. For anyone on the Buddhist path, I recommend *A Buddhist Journal: Guided Practices for Writers and Meditators* by Beth

Jacobs, PhD. (10) The clear guidance Beth provides helps us to move more deeply into our practice. She includes, for example, working with distractions, exploring our breathing, studying how the sense of self is constructed, ways to use and create a mantra, and much more. There is an exercise for responding to Dogen's essay, *Jijuyu Zammai*." Her exercise can take you deeper into that essay. Beth and I have practiced together and studied with Diane for over twenty years. Her writing exercises and insights into the journaling process are wonderful openings of "verbal pranja."

DISCOVERING DOGEN FOR YOURSELF

I asked a long-time senior student, Yuge Julia Pagenkopf, to write this section. Julia's dharma name, "Yuge," means "Freely Transforming." Her name mirrors Dogen's way of turning into the circle and being turned by the transformations of awakening. Many scholars have researched Dogen; Julia also does her research. Her insights born of personal practice and her suggestions can bring Dogen's teaching alive for you. Dogen's writing style is often convoluted and paradoxical. Don't give up; his depths are calling to yours.

DISCOVERING DOGEN
BY YUGE JULIA PAGENKOPF

As with most things in Zen, discoveries often have a serendipitous nature. They happen when the need arises. And so it was with my discovery of Dogen, which came about from two sources. The first arose from Dogen's use of poetic imagery to explain difficult concepts hidden in his use of mountains and rivers, or the boat. He writes: "... *the sky, the water, and the shore are all the boat's world ...*" (MD-85—other citations are given at the end of my essay). Or the plum blossom: "*When the old plum tree suddenly opens, the world of blossoming flowers arises.*" (MD-55) And "*The whole moon and even the whole sky are reflected in a drop of dew on a blade of grass.*" (RG-3) A particular favorite of mine is: "*When a fish swims, no matter how far it swims, it doesn't reach the end of the ocean. When a bird flies, no matter how high it flies, it cannot reach the end of the sky.*" (RG-4)

This is all very poetic language and, therefore, not easily under-stood. As an artist, I read the passages slowly and let my imagination create pictures in my mind to situate me within the scene. In a sense, I dive below the surface of the words, reading them over and over. In so much of his writings, Dogen is talking about the foundational Buddhist activity of enlightenment – and our intention to awaken. We can't reach enlightenment by thinking our way there. Awakening is not a rational activity; it is an experience. So I let myself experience what he is offering.

Walking through his blue mountains, I can sense the rock underfoot and the cool mountain air against my skin. Standing under the falling plum blossoms, I feel the dark pink, sweet-smelling petals on my upturned face. Swimming in the ocean, I respond to the flowing support of the water and the awareness of an endless horizon. I experience a passionate emotional response and the combination of opening myself up to the imagery and sensation helps me to 'see' his meaning, and 'feel' my way to his truth.

While my initial reading of Dogen's original works (in translation) sparked my imagination, full understanding (if that is ever possible with Dogen!) is very difficult. I appreciated the imagery and the precision with which Dogen uses nature metaphors to illustrate his thoughts, but I soon realized that additional study and other resources were going to be necessary to bring clarity to his writings and make his teachings come alive.

So I turned to Shohaku Okumura's book, *The Mountains and Waters Sutra: A Practitioner's Guide to Dogen's Sansuikyo,* and his book, *Realizing Genjo Koan: The Key to Dogen's Shobogenzo.* Both books are essential and I can't recommend them too highly.

The *Sansuikyo* essay is dense and the writing is compressed, pared down to its core. At the same time, it is loaded with descriptions and imagery that have hidden meanings. But Okumura does a wonderful job of explaining.

In this essay, Dogen says that we are the mountains walking and waters flowing. Mountains are huge, complete forms, seemingly permanent. And yet they are changing all the time—continuously "walking," as Dogen says, arising and arising, dharma gate to dharma gate—moment to moment—in complete interdependent origination with everything else. Dogen teaches us that this is how we live—in relationship with all beings, in complete connection with all beings, caught together in the web of inter-being. And therefore, we are immersed in the daily cause and effect of our interdependent lives— lives that we so often "walk" through unaware.

Okumura says, *"Another way of saying 'walking' might be the continuing unfolding of personal karma, life force, and evolution, even when we are not thinking about practice."* (MW-99)

Although we may not be thinking about practice, we are still making choices and decisions about our life every moment. Dogen suggests that these moments are exactly the present-moment of practice: to commit to awakening, to be open to those serendipitous seconds when the small self becomes aware of Buddhanature.

Dogen uses the mountains and waters as expressions for phenomena in which we live—manifestations of reality, of the 10,000 things. Our realities constantly interpenetrate one another. And what do the waters do? Water penetrates and changes form. Water dissolves and liberates. Water is form and emptiness. If we are mountains and waters, then we are form and change, constantly arising and transforming as bodhisattvas. The essay speaks to us about our bodhisattva vow to work with our self, and the reality our self creates. And the way we do that is to use the forms, or manifestations, in our lives—all the bits and pieces, the stories and experiences, the emotions, the joys and disappointments—to realize liberation.

Yet Dogen makes an important distinction about this liberation. He says that "conveying oneself toward all things to carry out practice-enlightenment is delusion." However, "all things coming and carrying out practice-enlightenment through the self is realization." (MW-47) In other words, reaching for enlightenment, trying to achieve realization as a goal, is delusion. In trying to reach a goal, we separate ourselves from the present, liberated moment. But letting life come to us, being present to life just as it manifests—that is realization. Not living in separation from all beings, but living together, interconnected, with all beings and whatever arises.

This point of "achievement" can be a particular area of practice for me—not grasping at a goal, not pushing myself toward a particular target, and then measuring myself in a negative way when I don't reach the goal I have artificially established. It's so easy to lapse into craving enlightenment, wanting to achieve that ultimate goal! This was especially true in my early years with Buddhism. I let my meditation practice become an exercise in achievement—if I sat very still, in silence, constantly stopping thought, every day, practice, practice,

practice, I would achieve enlightenment. Instead I got stiff muscles, a clenched jaw, and a sense that something wasn't right.

Expectations can be strong attachments that pull us out of our Buddhanature and take us away from the present moment. Expectations cause us to separate ourselves—I am this person now, but I really want to be that person who has... (*whatever*). We create a gap between the "me" now and "that me" in the future. I don't think that means that we shouldn't have goals. But it is important to understand the level of "attachment" we have placed on achieving those goals. What stories are we telling ourselves? How do we view ourselves? Do you see yourself as good, then bad, then good, then bad? Or just unskillful at times? How harsh we can be when judging ourselves, women in particular. I never used the word unskillful with regard to myself until I became a Buddhist and learned to drop my so called "original sinful" and over-achieving, spiritually striving self.

If we believe that we are caught, then we can take a step back and be enfolded, again and always, in loving Buddhanature, wisdom nature. We can step back into the stability and serenity of the mountains. As Dogen so beautifully explained, we live IN Buddhanature, not WITH Buddhanature. We ARE Buddhanature. So our practice continuously manifests Buddhanature and manifests the world—we are the fish in the ocean and the bird flying in the sky—we can never NOT BE in our element, in Buddhanature.

Okumura says, "The Buddha's teaching always has two sides: peacefully being still and always walking vigorously." (MW-195) Studying the essay helped me to see how my path was shaping me and my reality, that I was not in charge of the path. I saw the importance of "walking" the path in complete awareness of the present moment. There is no separation of ourselves and others, between form and emptiness, between space and time. Okumura describes Dogen's thinking: "If we practice sincerely, mindfully, and wholeheartedly,

Buddhahood is already here, in what we are doing right now, even though we have not yet crossed over to the other shore." (MW-68)

I find this teaching so wonderful! Every day, it is possible to wake up and realize we are already Buddhas—because we practice. We intentionally are aware of the choices we make and the karma we are creating. We mindfully immerse ourselves in the daily rhythms of our lives, of our relationships, our activities, our dreams. The immersion feels like an opening up of our mind and all our senses, as we become willing to accept the First Noble Truth, that our lives will include pain and suffering, as well as joy and happiness. Our practice is how we integrate that First Noble Truth in our lives and understand that we can increase or decrease that suffering by our choices. This is the radiance of practice/enlightenment.

The other source of my discovery of Dogen interconnects perfectly with Dogen's *Genjo Koan*. It is Shinshu Roberts' essay on Uji or "Being/Time" in *Receiving the Marrow: Teachings on Dogen by Soto Zen Women Priests*. This essay opened up for me an understanding of time as being and my being as time. I saw the correlation to practice/enlightenment and Buddhanature. Roberts says, "Buddha-nature is time/being itself." (RM-73) "Time and being exist together—in the particularity of life." (RM-90) Uji is inseparable from practice-enlightenment—and life/reality changes in every moment, constantly flowing. Time gives us a feeling of movement and change, just as the particulars of our life give meaningful shape to our form and reality. Practice enlightenment is occurring every moment as we live through, in, with all the forms—the dharma gates—of our daily lives. These forms are uniquely our own because we choose them, we each shape them and they in turn shape our path. Whether we are a teacher, parent, engineer, single mother, teenager, older adult in hospice care, the time we experience has meaning because our choices give our life meaning.

Entry Points and Skillful Means

To make meaningful choices requires awareness. In Dogen's *Genjo Koan*, there is repeated emphasis on the present moment and our attention to that moment. This really does take practice—the practice of constant awareness. It's like sitting in zazen all day and yet moving through the world.

Okumura says, "Each person's zazen influences everything in the world, everything reveals its own original realization, and the realization of all beings influences the person in zazen." (RG-201) So our zazen practice is critical. It is the underpinning to our entire practice. According to Okumura, Dogen did not see any difference "between practicing in the zendo and working in the world..." (RG-92) Practice realization is sitting on the zafu in zazen and as we go throughout our day—living, practicing, living, practicing—we never leave the cushion.

I find it helpful in strengthening the practice of awareness to take Dogen's "step backward." In his *Fukanzazengi*, he says:

> *You should therefore cease from practice based on intellectual understanding, pursuing words and following after speech, and learn the backward step that turns your light inwardly to illuminate yourself. Body and mind of themselves will drop away, and your original face will be manifest. If you want to attain suchness you should practice suchness without delay.*

For me, practicing suchness is asking questions: Where am I in this moment? What am I thinking in this moment? What/who am I aware of in this moment? What am I feeling? Questions help to bring me back to the present. Situating myself in the present brings my mind out of the future (where it likes to spend a lot of time planning!) so my awareness can rest in the present moment.

Being present also helps me be aware of the basic formations, or "*skandas*," mentioned in *The Heart Sutra*—forms, feelings, perceptions, habit formations, consciousnesses. What form is arising? What is my emotional response to the form? What is the perception/narrative I am creating around this emotion?

Practice realization can help us turn the five skandhas from weaknesses and stumbling blocks into strengths and wisdom gates. Through practice, life changes when you realize you are awakening every day. Dogen says, *"Realization does not destroy the person, as the moon does not make a hole in the water. The person does not obstruct realization, as a drop of dew does not obstruct the moon in the sky."* (RG-127) There is no separation from the life you are living and Buddhanature.

Dogen says in his *Maka Hannya Haramitsu*:

> *The whole body is prajna. All others [which include the self] are prajna. The whole self [which includes others] is prajna. The entire universe—east, west, south, and north —is prajna."* (RG-209)

We are the mountains walking, practicing/living our lives/our space— in interdependence with all beings every day. And we are the rivers, realizing/living in time—in constant change and impermanence. We are stable and we are flowing. We are relative and we are universal. It is a dance, really. We are all dancers. We are all constantly creating. Dogen writes *"...we give birth to life; life makes us into ourselves."* (MW-74)

Okumura comments, *"The world creates me and I create the world."* (MW-75) We are form; we are emptiness; we are possibility.

Allow yourself to be possible. Study Dogen. Read his words over and over, with patience. Live with his contradictions and his poetry, his apparent paradoxes and radiant images. Let your mind rest and allow your heart to take over understanding. Enlightenment is not logical! Liberation is experience. Awake every day in Buddhanature and be confident that you can meet with equanimity the sufferings, joys, surprises, hurts, the great sadnesses and the great loves that will be part of your path.

Essay Sources:

MD = Tanahashi, Kazuaki (Ed.): *Moon in a Dewdrop: Writings of Zen Master Dogen*. North Point Press, NY. 1985.

RG = Okumura, Shohaku: *Realizing Genjokoan*. Wisdom Publications, MA. 2010.

MW = Okumura, Shohaku: *The Mountains and Waters Sutra: A Practitioner's Guide to Dogen's "Sansuikyo."* Wisdom Publications, MA. 2018.

RM = Carney, Eido Frances (Ed.): *Receiving the Marrow: Teachings on Dogen by Soto Zen Women Priests*. Temple Ground Press, WA. 2012.

CONTEMPLATIVE DRAWING

If you are inclined to pick up a crayon, a marker, or a paintbrush, try contemplative drawing. It opens the soul so physical shapes and colors reveal hidden insights.

The practice described below is adapted from the book *Visual Journaling: Going Deeper Than Words* by Barbara Ganim and Susan Fox. (11) People usually respond enthusiastically. You may also find this practice, or your own version of contemplative drawing and painting, to be a vital part of your ongoing practice realization.

INSTRUCTIONS FOR CONTEMPLATIVE DRAWING:

PREPARATION: Set up a private workspace with crayons, markers, colored pencils, or paints and a large piece of blank paper at least 8½ x 11 inches. Take a few minutes to settle in your body. Then follow the steps below.

- Identify a situation (either a long-standing mind habit or a current issue in your life). Choose something you would like to understand better, to heal, or to see in a freer way. Write it out across the top of the paper.

- Close your eyes. Make an intention to stay mindfully present to what arises from within as you draw. When you are drawing, if your attention does wander, gently return to the practice. Recall the 3 Rs: **R**ecognize, **R**elease, **R**eturn.

- Open your eyes to gaze at the blank paper and wait until an inclination to draw begins to rise. Allow the colors to "choose themselves" as you begin drawing spontaneously. Let shapes, colors, lines, unrecognizable forms, scribbles, etc. come forth on the paper. Avoid thinking about making a recognizable picture. Allow the drawing to happen without analysis or critique. Stop when the process of drawing ends of itself.

Sit in silence with your drawing for a bit, then follow the eight prompts below. Simply wait and receive what arrives. It helps to write down these arisings. If nothing shows up, let the prompt go.

1. The drawing makes me feel ...

2. The drawing seems to be telling me ...

3. The color _____ feels . . . (continue with other significant colors)

4. I am disturbed by . . .

5. I like . . .

6. I am realizing that . . .

7. The request of the drawing could be ...

8. The title of the drawing is ...

When you know your practice with the drawing is concluded, offer your work for the healing of others. Finally, take some time to decide how you might follow through on the invitation that came to you from doing this practice. Consider how your thinking patterns, your words, your actions might change. What aspiration may be possible?

ENGAGING WITH POETRY

Writing a poem is not as daunting as it might seem. The format below gives you the cues to let a poem unfold. It is a "Diamond Poem," which I may have learned way back in grade school. Writing a diamond poem continues to be helpful—especially when sensing something needs to be turned around within you. When you know what that is, you are ready to begin.

- Draw the frame of a square with its points at the top and bottom of your paper. (See example below.)
- Write the topic of the poem at the top. Then continue as shown here.

The topic word(s)

Brief words describing the topic word(s).

A longer phrase, a question, a comment or an action

Two words to carry forward the middle phrase.

Repeat or transform the topic word.

Here's a sample diamond poem on the topic of losing a job:

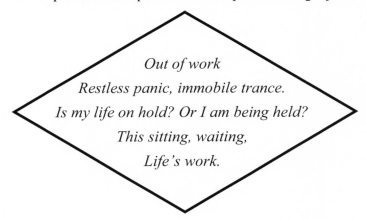

Out of work

Restless panic, immobile trance.

Is my life on hold? Or I am being held?

This sitting, waiting,

Life's work.

Much Zen poetry is as sparse and simple as a diamond poem, particularly the classic haiku form: First line, three or five syllables. Second line, five or seven syllables. Third line, three or five syllables. The following haiku was written by Mitsu Suzuki. She was married to Shunryu Suzuki Roshi. After he died in 1971, she continued teaching and writing poetry at the San Francisco Zen Center, living to be 102 years old.

Shells cast off
Cicadas silent
Morning breeze.
(12)

The simplicity of the haiku form might inspire you to write one yourself. A Dharma sister of mine, Myoshin Sheryl Lilke, wrote a poem styled after haiku for me after I broke my ankle. We were together on an autumn retreat at Ryumonji Monastery in Iowa. While the group was still asleep, I went out on the bell tower platform to see the stars. It was pitch dark so I could not see I had reached the end of the platform. Stepping off into open space—a nanosecond of flying before hitting the gravel six feet down. Sheryl's poem continues teaching me now. Notice how she adapts the traditional form.

Paula Wakes the Dragon
Bone snaps. Drum thumps. Bell rings in darkness.
All rise for a singular silence.
All pass away with the frost at dawn.

Another Japanese poetic form, *honkadori*, is a way to bring forth your own poetic soul with the help of another poet. You move into and through the poet's words and then wait to receive a response. First, choose a poem from an author whose poetry you love. Then:

- Divide a piece of lined paper vertically in half.
- Write out the poem, line by line, down one side of the piece of paper.
- Read line one slowly. Pause. Then in the space across from that line, write a response, a question, or an image that echoes that line.
- Continue this "call and response" for each line of the poem. Finally, fold over the original poem and read the poem it inspired you to create.

To practice "deep calling to deep," here are a few short poems by Dogen. Try working with them in the *honkadori* form. The poems are from Volume Ten of Dogen's *Extensive Record*.

Cool wind just blew through, awakening echoes of autumn.
The weather, refreshing and clear, bears new fruit.
Because new fruit, fragrance fills the world.
Where we cannot escape, we intimately hear. (#70)

In our lifetime, false and true, good and bad are confused.
While playing with the moon, scorning winds, listening to birds,
For many years I merely said the mountains had snow.
This winter, I suddenly realized that snow
completes the mountain. "(#90)

In the following poem, notice how Dogen points to and then reverses the relationship between practice and finding language for realization beyond expression.

Given to a Zen Person Asking for a Verse
"This mind itself is Buddha;
Practice is difficult, expounding it is easy.
No mind, no Buddha;
Expounding is difficult, practice is easy." (#63)

ENTRY POINTS AND SKILLFUL MEANS

Entry points for discovering the deep Mind are as diverse as we are. In general, there are three openings or "channels" to follow: your eyes open into images, your ears open into sound, and your body opens into touch and movement. There is much available online about these three channels: visual, auditory, and kinesthetic. Each provides access to the external world and the inner world.

Do you learn best by seeing something, by reading, by picturing images within? Does sound—the human voice, music, the sounds around you and in nature—grab your attention most strongly? Or do you favor bodily action, touch and movement to engage with your experience? Often the channels combine. Writing or making art is visual and kinesthetic.

What channel(s) do you most often use to access the outer world? The inner worlds? All three interact to skillfully support each other for practice realization. For example, my weakest channel is auditory. Just listening is tough. If I don't have a pen and paper for doodling (kinesthetic channel), I'll lose focus. When Diane gives her Dharma talks, I use my preferred channel—visual—to see words along with moving the pen across the paper—kinesthetic—in order to support my weaker auditory channel.

The Appendix offers examples of skillful means for entering practice from four Sophia Zen students. Three have found the visual and kinesthetic channels to be transformative. The fourth student practices with dance, which unites the auditory channel with kinesthetic discovery. If auditory skillful means is your preference, you may be drawn to chanting, hearing talks or poetry, or listening to music. Does speaking with someone—on the phone or face to face—reach you most deeply?

Of course, use your dominant, preferred channel(s). Then explore the unknown. The essays by Suzanne, Sandy, Pat, and Nancy are encouragements for self-discoveries beyond what we think we are. Your capacity is unlimited. Each of these students has been a teacher for me. I honor the awakenings they shine forth.

Please give yourself a lifetime to discover and rediscover how the depths of your own mystery call to you. Honor any and every way you begin to express your wholeness, your authenticity. The Bodhisattva of Compassion, Kuan Yin, is sometimes shown with 1,000 arms to signify the myriad ways we humans express our compassionate hearts. Each hand has the eye of wisdom, for these activities are not simply ego talents. Big Life lives through them.

How and where do you sense you being turned by Big Life? In the garden? At the bedside of an ill person? Writing your congressperson? Feeding a child? Listening to a friend? Caring for an animal?

Each intentional choice creates the energy of evolution. Each of us moves the Great Turning uniquely. Thus the world awakes.

Notes to Chapter Five

(1) *New York Times Magazine*, August 15, 2021, p12.

(2) *Poetry of Presence: An Anthology of Mindfulness Poems.* Edited by Phyllis Cole-Dai and Ruby R. Wilson, Grayson Books, West Hartford, CT, 2017.

(3) *The Great Work: Our Way into the Future.* Bell Tower, New York, 1999, p7, p201.

(4) *Awakened Cosmos: The Mind of Classical Chinese Poetry*, Shambhala Publications, Boston, 2019, pp107-109.

(5) *The Art of Just Sitting: Essential Writings on the Zen Practice of Shikantaza.* Edited by John Daido Loori, Wisdom Publications, Boston, 2002.

(6) *New York Times* interview, August 9, 2020.

(7) *The Pregnant Virgin.* Inner City Books, Toronto, p85.

(8) I find it helpful to remember that 95% of the Universe is dark matter and energy. Inquiry arising from the Deep Mind cannot always be perceived by the surface mind. Likewise, the Universal Deep Mind's continuous response is beyond our capacity to perceive. See Dogen's text in the Appendix, p143.

(9) See also Hee-Jin Kim's excellent book, *Dogen on Meditation and Thinking: A Reflection on His View of Zen*, Chapter 4 "The Reason of Words and Letters." SUNY, 2007.

(10) *A Buddhist Journal: Guided Practices for Writers and Meditators* by Beth Jacobs, North Atlantic Books, Berkeley, 2018.

(11) *Visual Journaling: Going Deeper than Words* by Barbara Ganim and Susan Fox. Quest Books, Wheaton, IL, 1991.

(12) *White Tea Bowl: 100 Haiku for 100 Years of Life.* Shambhala Publications, Boulder, 2014, p93.

CHAPTER SIX

TURNING AND BEING TURNED CONTINUOUSLY

"But already my desire and my will were being turned
like a wheel, all at one speed, by the Love which
moves the sun and the other stars."
—Dante Alighieri, *The Paradiso*, Canto 33

ARE WE THERE YET?

R estless children on a long trip cry, "Are we there yet? Are
we there yet?" We too yearn for the fulfillment of our
aspirations. I imagine Dogen reminding us "...between
aspiration, practice, enlightenment and nirvana, there is never a
moment's gap." Continuous practice" collapses linear time. All
the turns of the circle of the way are happening simultaneously. In
a talk on Essay #39, Zoketsu Norman Fischer says:

*This is a very radical and thoroughgoing thought from
Dogen. Think about it. There are no marks, no
boundaries, no definitions of continuous practice, because
continuous practice is exactly life itself. But it's more than
that. Continuous practice includes death. It includes non-
existence too. Whatever you or anyone else would impose
from outside...Life is pure, and it is whole so there is
nothing to force here.* (1)

Nothing to force, to drive, to push from here to there because there is nowhere to go and no attainment to accomplish. Yet simultaneously in linear life, wholehearted commitment is required. Perseverance is required. Consider a toddler learning to walk. Forcing the child to walk across the room usually does not work. The child's instinctive perseverance probably will. Can you think of an example in your life where you felt the difference between forcing yourself to finish a task and being present in the process? How was the energy different? Which approach lends itself to not giving up on yourself?

Essay #18, *Dharma Blossoms Turn Dharma Blossoms*, is a challenge to study but it holds the heart of Dogen's practice realization teaching. A flower does not force itself to bloom and bear fruit. It naturally responds to the causes and conditions of its situation. As it turns itself toward the sun, it is also being turned into blooming. The bud's turning is its "practice." Its blossoming is "realization." Both are occurring simultaneously.

Your continuous practice is always already realization. Realization is continuously practicing. *Don't wait for great enlightenment, as great enlightenment is the tea and rice of daily activity...Love and respect your body, mind, and self that are engaged in continuous practice.* In these few words from *Continuous Practice*, Dogen collapses all separation between spirit and matter, eternity and this moment.

HOW DOES THE DHARMA TURN YOU?

Recall that Dogen always reminds us not to split our relative experience from Universal reality. In Essay #43, *The Moon*, Dogen teaches that your choice to practice in your small, ordinary bits of the physical world is being turned by the "big thing" of enlightened realization. Consider experiencing the moon.

The moon often is a symbol for the experience of enlightenment. Dogen insists: don't use the physical moon as a spiritual symbol. Don't make the moon an object; don't make enlightenment something "other" than your physical world.

Rather, the moon, in and of itself, is "Moon Thusness." Any ordinary, physical experience can be Thusness arising in our awareness. There is no "holier" meaning beyond it.

All things are buddha things. And not just lovely things like the moon, the rose, or the lotus. Even the stick the monks use to wipe their bottoms is a buddha in some koans. Try asking yourself, "Where is buddha?" as you move through the day. Let yourself be surprised by whatever shows up. Stop in your tracks with wide-eyed immediacy.

In Essay #18, Dogen works with the metaphor of flowering to teach the reciprocity of being turned and turning the Wheel of Dharma. First he states, "When your mind is deluded, you are turned by dharma blossoms." Dogen is not criticizing us for being deluded. Instead, he kindly telling us to be intimate with our deluded thoughts. "Without making mistake after mistake, one departs from the Way." (Essay #6 *This Very Mind is Buddha*) A delusion is a mistaken perception. In any deluded mis-take, there is a pivot for being turned around. Any dharma that arises is a tipping point. We can wobble and regress into suffering or we can stand upright and choose liberation.

The microscopic coronaviruses are dharmas blossoming in order to survive. In response, our interdependent behaviors result in macro consequences. How we choose to think, speak, and act in response to any cataclysmic emergency is an opportunity to "emerge" awake. Humankind can turn into the light of Wisdom, just as flowers naturally turn to the sun. The human heart can create an Earth community blossoming with compassion.

Recall Macy's request (p. 75) "to be fully present to what is happening in the world." When fully present, we see pivot points for conversion on the spot. Perhaps a person special to you breaks a promise. Or you feel despair when you watch the news. You need not repeat your habitual reaction. In the silent stillness, I recall this teaching: "Consumed with anger, the world is an ugly place. Bathed in kindness, the world is a wonderful place. But ah, the same world!" What dissolves can evolve. A loving response is always possible. Do you agree?

Can we trust the possibility of love no matter what? Buddha nature is no longer dormant in the nanosecond we choose to stop being turned by fear and afflictive habits. If we are intimately present with whatever is arising, buddha seeds can blossom.

Wisdom knows the basic goodness of everything that's occurring. "She does not stray away from it." (*Hymn to the Perfection of Wisdom*) Wisdom does not abandon us to the forces of fear. She asks only for aware presence. That we do not abandon the Self we do not yet know.

In Catholic school, we were told to avoid the "near occasions of sin." We were warned that an R-rated movie would lead us into sin. Zen's path is not avoidance or repression of a predictable "tempting" habit, but rather mindful awareness. As we stay present and aware in radical intimacy, the habit can be the "near occasion" of grace. "Thus do not resent delusion," says Dogen. "If you were not intimate with yourself, you would resent yourself." Remember, for Dogen, enlightenment is intimacy with all things. We can contrive many excuses to avoid intimacy with whatever is going on. Even so, the buddha embryo is present, uncontrived and open in effortless receptivity.

HOW DO YOU TURN THE DHARMA?

Much of the time, we feel insignificant. How could my little life change the course of evolution? Besides, we want to see results for our efforts. Gandhi knew this. He asked his followers to do seemingly insignificant things: spin their own cloth, march to claim free salt from the ocean. They did not know what could result. Let's return to Dogen's Essay #18, *Dharma Blossoms Turn Dharma Blossoms*, to explore this question of insignificance:

> *When your mind is enlightened, you turn the dharma blossoms. That is to say, when the dharma blossoms fully turn you are empowered to turn the dharma blossoms. While the original turning never stops, you return to turn the dharma blossoms. This is the single great matter manifesting here and now...Emptiness is form is the turning of dharma beyond birth and death...Rejoice! From eon to eon there have been dharma blossoms.*

Dogen's writing requires slow re-readings to unravel his teaching. It might help to place his insights in the context of current cosmology. Dogen is saying your aspiration to blossom arises from the creative energy of the cosmos, the "original turning." Today, we might say enlightenment is originally coded into the function of the Universe as its promise or vow to all beings. Emptiness births forms of ever more diverse and complex buddhas.

Brian Swimme's words about the wonder of evolution are simple: "The Earth was once molten rock and now it sings opera!"

Science can now study the code of DNA in human life. I suggest human DNA holds the code of continuous practice realization. Buddhist scholar Paula Arai writes:

> *"DNA is the record of interrelatedness that spans billions of years and connects all life forms; it provides evidence that we are not independent entities. Humans share DNA with ancient bacteria, grains of rice, cherry trees, butterflies, baboons and frogs. Each of our cells contains the code of our interrelated web of life. This biological phenomena of interbeing is consistent with the teaching of The Heart Sutra...Which genes will be expressed, however, depends on numerous causes and conditions and actions in the present moment. (2)*

We can ignore the enlightenment coded into our nature. We can also awaken in our diverse forms of consciousness. Activating the enlightened coding we share with all beings describes a Universe aware of Itself through us.

You and I, eight billion other humans, and innumerable other species are alive at this specific moment of evolution. Consider the "clock" of human time of the past 240,000 years in a single day. In the last 20 seconds before midnight (i.e., since 1950), we have used up more resources and fuel than in all of human history. (3) Because our culture is not yet awake, we are like the *Titanic*, moving very quickly but heading for a crash.

Records indicate there was not enough time to change the trajectory of the *Titanic*. Disaster was inevitable. As the succinct practice saying puts it: "Pain is inevitable in human life. But suffering is optional..." —because we can choose how we respond to pain. The painful experience will continue if we add thoughts of worry or anger or despair. What about the heart*minds of the individual passengers and crew on the

Titanic? Did anyone choose to turn from panic and fear toward trust and kindness? Our moment of humanity is at this pivot point. An irreversible chain reaction of the effects of climate change could be set in motion. We are all in the same boat, carried by something more unfathomable than ourselves. We cannot know future results. If we want to predict the future, look for it in the choices of the present.

GRATITUDE

Gratitude for the gift of life is the primary wellspring of all religions, the hallmark of the mystic, the source of all true art ... It is a privilege to be alive in this time when we can choose to take part in the self-healing of the world.
—Joanna Macy

Joanna expresses gratitude for the possibility of choice. If we choose to practice, we say, "Yes, I am open, I am willing, to be turned around continuously. We are take part in the Great Turning.

When anger grips my jaw or fear clutches my belly...when tears well up, I choose to stand in my personal pivot point.

Over and over, I hear Dogen's *Genjo Koan* helping me not to ignore awakening: "Small things are big things in disguise." The small thing is to recognize and release the urge to react to fear by starting a story line. What is the immense thing? Buddha nature Awakening! I imagine Dogen cheering us on: "Your continuous practice of this day is the seed of all buddhas and the practice of all buddhas."

At the conclusion of a Zen sangha practice, we affirm our intention to actualize buddha nature by taking the four Bodhisattva vows:

> *Beings are numberless; I vow to save them. Delusions are inexhaustible; I vow to end them. Dharma gates are boundless; I vow to enter them. The Buddha Way is unsurpassable; I vow to become it.*

These vows are the practice of all buddhas yet we speak the "I" pronoun. We offer our vows, knowing they are impossible if we depend on our egos to carry them out. In Yuge Julia's essay "Discovering Dogen," she notes how Dogen honors interdependence. In *Genjo Koan,* he says we are deluded if we carry ourselves forward to save all beings. But if the myriad things experience themselves through us, the Big Life of enlightening energy can work through us. A cause for gratitude, humility, and confidence.

Reb Anderson was a student of Shunryu Suzuki, like Diane. Sophia Zen students study his book, *Being Upright: Zen Meditation and the Bodhisattva Precepts,* before they publicly take the Bodhisattava vows. (4)

These words of Reb's inspire my gratitude for our moment of practice realization:

> *All things are so deeply connected that at the precise moment when you are just yourself the whole Universe is just itself. When you realize yourself the entire universe is just itself. When you realize yourself, all things are realized. Being realized, you are liberated from suffering...and all beings are liberated (202). Anybody who is herself completely will be a revolutionary. There has never been anything like you being yourself before... this transforms, this turns the wheel of dharma, and this happens in the midst of fierce flames that surround you (200).*

May we be grateful, not afraid, to be revolutionaries by being our full liberated selves.

I began this handbook by thanking you for joining me in this way of practice realization. We are receiving each other's "subtle mutual assistance." Dogen honors the assistance we receive from everything, no exceptions:

> *... trees, grasses, walls and fences expound and exalt the Dharma for the sake of ordinary people, sages and all living beings* [though such help is] *"beyond ordinary perception." (Jijuyu Zammai).*

I offer a story from Joanna Macy about trees and fences that illustrates Dogen's teaching.

Sometime after the Chernobyl nuclear plant disaster in 1986, Joanna visited with the Ukrainian people living in nearby villages to lead a "Despair and Empowerment" training. She came with no expectation that her work could make a difference in healing their devastated lives. She simply stayed with the people, listened to their pain and feelings of abandonment. They told her how they'd often approach the fence erected to separate them from the elm tree forest that had been a part of their community life. They came to the fence to mourn. By tending to their grief, they were gradually able to be turned to creating beauty: a circle dance they now do as they chant in gratitude for the elms. Dancing and singing sustained their reciprocal relationship with the forest. The people taught the dance to Joanna. She promised she would teach the dance everywhere as she travelled the world.

In 2012, when Joanna concluded her practice intensive at Holy Wisdom Monastery in Madison, Wisconsin, we danced "The Elm Dance"—over 80 people circling forward, in reverse, and then forward; moving into the center point together and out to the edges. Now I am grateful to be able to teach the "The Elm Dance" with many different groups. That fence, those trees, and the villagers continue to expound and exalt the Dharma.

Turning and Being Turned

On February 24, 2022, those living near the Chernobyl site experienced another disaster—military invasion. I am confident people worldwide are energizing goodness, moving the force of Wisdom, invoking the power of peace.

Dogen's proclamations in *Jijuyu Zammai* are happening within us even now as we …

> … *turn round and round the teaching of original enlightenment, all who dwell and talk together with them also join with one another in possessing the inexhaustible, unceasing, incomprehensible and immeasurable Buddha Dharma, inside and outside throughout the Universe.*

In contrast to Dogen's exuberance, Meister Eckhart has a sparse way of expressing gratitude for the privilege of being alive:

> *If the only prayer you say in your entire life is 'Thank you,' that would be sufficient.* (5)

But not only a one-time thank you, Dogen might say to his Dominican brother:

> *Continuous Practice, day by day, is the most appropriate way of expressing gratitude.*

Dogen gives us his preferred way of saying farewell (Essay #46): "Please treasure yourself."

In the Buddhist tradition, we conclude a retreat or ceremony by expressing gratitude. Our gratitude takes the form of dedicating any merit that resulted from our practice realization to others. Now, as we conclude this handbook, I invite you to dedicate the merit of your work with the following intentions:

- May the merit of our practice be dedicated to the realization of the inherent Goodness we share with all beings.

146

- May we treasure each other as we protect the air, lands, waters, the plants, and animals of this beautiful Earth.

- May our aspiration to live into the Great Turning as love and wisdom be fulfilled.

It is already so. May we live as such.

Notes to Chapter Six

(1) Everyday Zen Foundation, June 19, 2010. everydayzen.org/
teachings/2010.

(2) *Painting Enlightenment: Healing Visions of the Heart Sutra*, Shambhala
Publications, Boulder, 2019, pp36-37.

(3) For specific analyses, see *Active Hope: How to Face the Mess We're In
Without Going Crazy.*

(4) Rodmell Press, Berkeley, 2001.

(5) Fox, p34.

APPENDIX

THE HEART SUTRA
(THE MAHA PRAJNA PARAMITA HRIDAYA SUTRA)

Avalokiteshvara bodhisattva when practicing deeply the prajna paramita perceived that all five skandhas are empty and was saved from all suffering and distress.

"O Shariputra, form does not differ from emptiness; that which is emptiness, form. The same is true of feelings, perceptions, habit formations, consciousnesses.

O Shariputra, all dharmas are marked with emptiness; they do not appear nor disappear, are neither tainted nor pure, do not increase or decrease.

Therefore, in emptiness, no form, no feelings, no perceptions, no habit formations, no consciousnesses, no eyes, no ears, no nose, no tongue, no body, no mind; no color, no sound, no smell, no taste, no touch, no object of mind; no realm of eyes and so forth until no realm of mind consciousness; no ignorance and also no extinction of it, and so forth until no old age and death and also no extinction of them; no suffering, no origination, no stopping, no path, no cognition, also no attainment.

With nothing to attain, the bodhisattva depends on prajna paramita and the mind is no hindrance. Without any hindrance no fears exist; far apart from every inverted view the bodhisattva dwells in nirvana.

In the three worlds all Buddhas depend on prajna paramita and attain unsurpassed complete perfect enlightenment.

Therefore know the prajna parmita is the great transcendent mantra, is the great bright mantra, is the utmost mantra, is the supreme mantra, which is able to relieve all suffering and is true, not false. So proclaim the prajna paramita mantra, proclaim the mantra that says:

"GATE, GATE, PARAGATE, PARASAMGATE!
BODHI! SVAHA!"

HYMN TO THE PERFECTION OF WISDOM

Homage to the Perfection of Wisdom, the lovely, the holy. The Perfection of Wisdom gives light. Unstained, the entire world cannot stain her. She is a source of light and from everyone in the triple world, she removes darkness. Most excellent are her works. She brings light so that all fear and distress may be forsaken, and disperses the gloom and darkness of delusion. She herself is an organ of vision. She has a clear knowledge of the own being of all dharmas, for she does not stray away from it. The Perfection of Wisdom of the Buddhas sets in motion the Wheel of the dharma.

JIJUYU ZAMMAI – EIHEI DOGEN

(Included in Essay #1, *On the Endeavor of Way*)

Ancestors and Buddhas, who have maintained the Buddha Dharma, all have held that practice based upon proper sitting in zazen in jijuyu samadhi was the right path through which their enlightenment opened. In India and China, those who have gained enlightenment have all followed in this way of practice. It is based upon the right transmission of the wonderful means in private encounter from master to disciple, and their receiving and maintaining of its authentic essence.

According to the authentic tradition of Buddhism, the Buddha Dharma, transmitted rightly and directly from one to another, is the supreme of the supreme. From the first time you meet your master and receive the teaching, you have no need for incense offerings, homage paying, nembutsu, penance disciplines, or silent sutra readings; only cast off body and mind in zazen.

When even for a short period of time you sit properly in samadhi, imprinting the Buddha-seal in your three activities (deeds, words, and thoughts), each and every thing excluding none is the Buddha-seal, and all space without exception is enlightenment. Accordingly, it makes Buddha-tathagatas all increase the Dharma joy of their original source, and renew the adornments of the way of enlightenment.

Then, when all classes of all beings in the ten directions of the universe – the hell dwellers, the hungry ghosts, and animals; the fighting demons, humans and devas – all together at one time being bright and pure in body and mind, realize the stage of absolute emancipation and reveal their original aspect, at that time all things together come to realization in themselves of the true enlightenment of the Buddha, utilize the Buddha-body, immediately leap the confines of this personal enlightenment, sit properly beneath the kingly tree of enlightenment, turn simultaneously the great and utterly incomparable Dharma-wheel, and expound the ultimate and profound prajna free from all human agency.

Since, moreover, these enlightened ones in their turn enter into the way of imperceptible mutual assistance, the person in zazen without fail casts off body and mind, severs the heretofore disordered and defiled thoughts and views emanating from his discriminating consciousness, conforms totally in himself to the genuine Buddha Dharma, and assists universally in performing the work of Buddhas at each of the various places the Buddha-tathagatas teach, that are as infinitely numberless as the smallest atom particles – imparting universally the *ki* transcending Buddha, vigorously uplifting the Dharma transcending Buddha. Then the land, the trees and grasses, fences, walls, tiles and pebbles, all the various things in the ten directions, perform the work of Buddhas.

Because of this, all persons who share in the wind and water benefits thus produced receive the unperceived help of the Buddha's wonderful and incomprehensible teaching and guidance, and all manifest their inherent enlightenment. Since all who receive and employ this fire and water turn round and round the teaching of original enlightenment, all who dwell and talk together with them also join with one another in possessing the inexhaustible, unceasing, incomprehensible, and immeasurable Buddha Dharma, inside and outside throughout the universe. Yet such things are not mingled in the perceptions of one sitting in zazen, because this occurs in the stillness of samadhi beyond human artifice, and is in itself realization. If practice and realization were two different stages as ordinary people consider them to be, the one sitting in zazen and things should perceive each other. To be associated with perceptions is not the mark of realization, because the mark of realization is to be beyond such illusions.

Moreover, although in realization the mind of the zazen practitioner and its objects both arise and disappear within the stillness of samadhi, since this occurs within the sphere of jijuyu, it does not disturb a single mote of dust, nor infringe upon a single phenomenon. It does great and wide-ranging buddha work, and performs the exceedingly profound recondite activities of preaching and enlightening. The trees, grasses, and the land involved in this all emit a bright and shining light, and preach the profound and incomprehensible Dharma; and it is endless. Trees and grasses, wall and fence expound and exalt the Dharma for the sake of ordinary people, sages and all living beings. Ordinary people, sages and all living beings in turn preach and exalt the Dharma for the sake of trees, grasses, wall and fence. The dimension of self-enlightenment qua enlightening others is basically replete with the characteristics of realization, and causes the principle of realization unceasingly.

Because of this, when even just one person, at one time, sits in zazen, they become imperceptibly one with each of all the myriad things, and permeate completely all time, so that within the limitless universe, throughout, past, future, and present, they are performing the eternal and ceaseless work of guiding beings to enlightenment. It is, for each and every thing, one and the same undifferentiated practice, and undifferentiated realization. Only this is not limited to the practice of sitting alone; the sound that issues from the striking of emptiness is an endless and wondrous voice that resounds before and after the fall of the hammer. And this is not all the practice of zazen does. Each and every thing is, in its original aspect, provided original practice – it cannot be measured or comprehended.

SKILLFUL MEANS OFFERED BY SOPHIA ZEN SANGHA STUDENTS

CREATING A MANDALA
BY KANJI SUZANNE MOYNIHAN

Creating a mandala is like meditating: you are engaging in a dance with Mystery, intentionally participating in a cosmic turning, a transformative process. In the making of a mandala, your sacred unique evolution becomes a visible treasure.

The word *mandala* is a Sanskrit term that means "circle." A mandala can be defined in two ways: externally as a schematic visual representation of the universe and internally as a guide for several psychophysical practices that take place in many Asian traditions, including meditation. If you wish to learn more, see **https://www.ancient.eu/mandala/.**

I've been intrigued ever since I took a meditation class on mandala-making. Just to put on paper an insight, an intention, a symbol of gratitude in an artistic form, affirms and strengthens something deep in me that yearns to make itself known. Mandalas have even helped me deal with problematic relationships and internal struggles. One time, I realized that I had a storm of self-negating thoughts running through my mind—like old tapes—so I fashioned an image of my head at the center of the mandala circle, then wrote down in a circular form around that drawing all of those unconscious beliefs that were having a heyday, better known as a hefty portion of my delusion. Just facing them gave me a sense of freedom. I experienced more clarity having faced my demons. I knew I could let go.

Although the traditional creation of mandalas involves intricate rites, you can create your own ritual. All you need is a quiet, solitary space, a few simple materials like an inexpensive drawing pad, a set of watercolor markers, colored pencils, a pen or whatever art materials you prefer. Usually white paper works best; black paper highlights unique shading and is also an option. No drawing experience is necessary. Other creative modes are sand or stone. Once on retreat, I drew a mandala in the driveway dirt! I have also visited stone mandalas left by a previous visitor as I reflectively walked on paths at a retreat center.

These are some basic points which have helped me and may also assist you as you initiate this practice in your life:

- **YOUR SACRED TIME:** You can do a mandala any time you feel inspired, for example, during your reserved meditation time or on retreat or some rainy afternoon or upon noticing an interior shift. Some practitioners create mandalas at regularly scheduled times, once a week. Sunday morning for me is a sacred time and usually begins with the creation of a mandala expressing itself in whatever forms it chooses. My intention is to let arise what lies deep within me into a visible form and then let it speak a new truth.

- **BEGINNING:** Draw a circle—any size you wish. You can make it as large or as small as you wish and may want to vary the size from time to time. A lunch plate or the top of a 32-oz. yogurt container are handy household items and would serve your purpose well. Then give yourself a few moments of quiet. Breathe. Enter into Silence. Allow your intention to arise. Sophia awaits to guide you. Images will come as you enter more deeply into the process.

- **DESIGN:** Follow your intuition as you decorate the perimeter of the circle. You might be drawn to use varied colored patterns around the edge or just a thick line in a singular color to strengthen the perimeter. This boundary secures the sacredness of your mandala

156

practice. As you move to your drawing, begin with a color that chooses you. Whatever initial image comes to you, just let go and trust it. Let your sacred intuition guide you. Whether it is a line, a streak across your circle, a symbol, or a more realistic image, enjoy the blossoming.

- **PROCESS:** Continue with other colors, other shapes. Listening to the quiet voice within, do whatever you are prompted to do, trusting the unfolding. No need to be concerned about the surface look. Your intention is to listen to your deepest Self. In the process of creating your mandala, your fears and anxieties, your gifts and joys are being gently brought to light. Mandalas reveal to you the beauty of your Deepest Self, your Buddha nature as you meet your fears, pain and sorrow in your unique ongoing process of liberation.

- **UPON FINISHING:** You will know you have completed your mandala when it feels right to you to stop drawing. Once completed, it is helpful to write the date and the meaning of the mandala outside of the circle. You may also wish to give it a title as one would a poem.

- **CONCLUDING RITUAL:** Then take a few moments to give thanks for the insights, the symbols, the coloring instruments, the revelation you experienced. Bow to your mandala as part of your ritual. Place it in an honored setting where you may wish to honor its message on a daily basis. Whatever your content, it serves to affirm you of your ongoing liberation, your enlightenment. You have completed an ancient sacred practice, a significant step in your awakening process.

Photography as a Contemplative Practice
by Sandy Wojtal-Weber

Photography has been a great love of my life for more than forty years. Over time, it has evolved from being a tool to document family events and travel to commercial work. Its current incarnation is most precious and real in my life. It has become a contemplative practice.

Experiencing the outdoors has always been a major activity in my life, whether it be backpacking in the mountains, camping with friends, hiking in the state and national parks, kayaking, or cross-country skiing. At some point, these moments in the natural world became more than just outdoor activities. I began to experience somatically and emotionally the profound beauty of these moments. One of my spiritual teachers, James Finley, described these as "moments of spontaneous contemplative experience," moments in which one is "interiorly quickened." I began to explore how I could experience more of these moments, which are ephemeral, coming, and going, with one returning to one's unawakened self.

I began carrying my camera on walks in nature and found myself stopping, pausing, noticing—just being absorbed for brief moments at a time. The photographs I made during those periods were somewhat different than the ones I usually take in that I did not spend much "thinking time" considering lighting, angle, composition, etc. The images were taken before the mind could interrupt and dictate what action to take.

In trying to understand what I was experiencing I did some research on different approaches which were not conventional ways of taking photos and found a category called Mindful Photography. Researching a bit further I found a practice, which originated in the Shambhala Community with Buddhist Teacher Chogyam Trungpa, known as *Miksang*. Miksang is a Tibetan

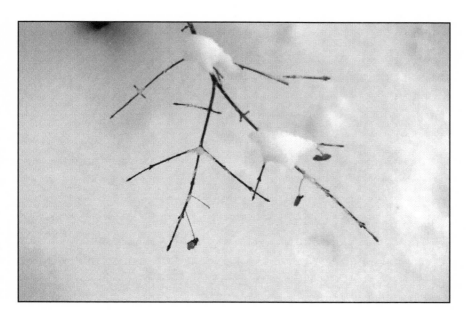

word for "Good Eye." I have since become a Level 1 *Miksang* teacher.

What is so beautiful about a contemplative approach to photography is that it is open to anyone. Everything you need is right here in this body, mind and heart. One of my teachers, Michael Wood, described the outcome of the contemplative practice this way: "The wisdom of this tradition is seeing your world and your life in a very awake way—it is not making beautiful images." Though having said this, my experience is that the images created during this practice are often very powerful. The images often evoke a response that this awareness, this moment is precious, this is real, and this is holy.

What follows is an abbreviated and adaptive exercise in mindful seeing. The premise for the exercise is that we make our world so familiar we do not see it anymore. Often we are in autopilot getting from one place to another and if asked what we saw along the way, we could not answer. I have broken it down to four steps or stages: Gazing, Receiving, Resting, and Creating.

Appendix

Contemplative Photography Practice

Four-Step Practice: Gazing—Receiving—Resting—Creating
Note: This practice can be done indoors or outdoors. I will describe it here as being done outdoors on a walk.

Preliminary Practice: This is a brief dropping into your surroundings. Noticing where your awareness is. Noticing what is happening in your body and taking several deep breaths in and out before you begin the practice. Spend five minutes doing this.

1) **Gazing:** As you walk, just observe, notice shapes, colors, texture, light, and shadow. You are not looking for something to photograph, you are just noticing.

2) **Receiving:** Begin to notice if anything "stops" you, catches your eye, causes you to pause for a moment. This pause in *Miksang* practice is known as a "gap" in thinking or a "flash of perception," which is a fresh, open moment, which does not last long. It is the time prior to the thinking mind labeling and filtering into likes and dislikes. This usually happens suddenly. So doing this practice regularly will help sensitize one to recognizing these moments. Do not pick up the camera or phone to take a photo immediately when you are "stopped."

3) **Resting:** Stay with the image that stopped you for a while and notice what or if the image evokes a feeling response. It may or may not. Continue observing a bit longer.

4) **Creating:** Taking your camera or cell phone, decide what is in the frame and what is out. What is a part of your original perception and include only that if possible. Take one photo and move on.

   Note: You may have numerous experiences on your walk.

For examples of photos that illustrate this practice, see my website, **www.capturelightphoto.com**.

SoulCollage® as a Spiritual Practice
by Ryujin Pat Shutts

SoulCollage® is a worldwide movement for self-discovery. It is creating a deck of cards through collaging images that reflect various aspects of your soul—your personality, gifts, loves, beliefs about life, areas of struggle and shadow, our deep goodness and beauty; as well as realizations that challenge and encourage and honoring all who assist you in life. It is an intuitive process in which one is often surprised by what each card has to say.

SoulCollage® was founded by Seena Frost when working on a program with Jean Houston, international teacher and founder of the Human Potential Movement in the late 1980s. Seena was a psychologist who was into Jungian psychology, archetypes, and was open to many spiritualities and cultures. She created this process for women's retreats. The process grew and grew in popularity and is used in various settings. It is very popular with art therapists and counselors. More information about SoulCollage® can be found at the website Soulcollage.com and in Seena's book, SoulCollage® Evolving.

I have led sessions at the Siena Retreat Center in Racine, Wisconsin for about 13 years. I have been trained as a SoulCollage® facilitator. I know this process is a way for people to get in touch with what is going on within themselves in a creative, fun, and yet very deep and meaningful way. It is like journaling with images but allowing our deeper selves/Spirit speak to us, teach us.

I attended my first SoulCollage® in the early 2000s. It was a very powerful experience—a celebration of my life and my journey. My first cards were not so great artistically, but still have great meaning to me. Here's what we do in our sessions, or you can do at home. First, we collect images and pictures we are drawn to—I get these pictures from everything: personal photos, magazines, books, old greeting cards, calendars, etc. You will need good glue, sharp small scissors, 5 x 8 inch-matt board cards (or any heavier paper or cardboard).

In this process, Seena stressed the power of an Egyptian belief that everything in the Universe is working for our benefit to help us and teach us. Those images you intuitively chose have something to say to you. It is good to glue to a background and then carefully cut out the other images. Then your creation looks like one unified card.

Try to keep each card to one theme. Don't try to put your whole life on one card. My theory is how it looks is not as important as what it means to you. It is your soul speaking. It is more about process than product. These cards are for you and can be made for others. They are not to be sold.

After you create your card, spend some time with it. The SoulCollage® tradition is to look at your card and say, "I am the One who…" "What do you want to say to me?"

For example, the first card I ever made was of a little girl in a garden in joyful awe of a ladybug. "I am the one who wants to have my eyes open for all the depths of life and not miss a thing- to see with contemplative eyes." The card was about noticing- really noticing—paying attention and seeing the deeper truths of life.

You can journal about your card. We are encouraged not to use words or write on our cards. They may have another message another day. I and many of the participants over the years have had many "Aha!" moments—deep realizations—honoring our life with all its struggles, glories, healings, and learnings. Doing this in a trusted community can be a very powerful experience of sharing what is really important in our lives. We always close the day with a "I Am the One Who…Circle" where we share one or two of our cards.

At our workshops, I make a few cards to share with the group, last summer I did a small retreat and did a few cards. I have a favorite picture of me at three months old. I had lost it and found it at the time of this retreat. I thought I want to make a SoulCollage® card with it. It was so fun!! I felt so much energy doing this card. I have this very suspicious look on my face and my fists are clinched…protecting my little three-month-old self. I found a background that looked like a rough texture and picture of a sparrow, which is very meaningful to me.

I have this card in my office. It is a reminder to me to unclutch—to stop fighting life. It reminds me of the inner healing that has happened in my life and is still happening as I learn to relax into my life one moment at a time. "I am the One who says 'Little Pat, just relax!'"

What do you do with your cards? There are various ways to use your cards…I usually have them on my prayer table or places to remind me of their messages. I love to meditate at Lake Michigan in the morning—on my desk at home, I have a card of Buddhist monks meditating at sunrise. Some people do readings with them, pulling two or three cards, asking what they have to say to them today.

At this point, I have at least 70 cards. Many of them have reoccurring themes. These are the deep parts of my soul that want to be expressed at this time or that I need to be in touch with. I have a lot of dolphins and Mary embracing the Christ Child and blue herons—all symbols to my soul.

I love doing SoulCollage® cards. It is a creative process that is simple and can be life-changing and affirming. Seena calls her book SoulCollage®Evolving. She believes that we are evolving the planet as we listen to our souls. May it be.

APPENDIX

MOVING FROM WITHIN
BY NYOBU NANCY SHINNERS

HOW MY DANCING BECAME A SPIRITUAL PRACTICE

The joy of dancing was instilled in me while dancing with my mother in our kitchen. I loved to dance at weddings and festivals. As I matured, I danced at home, often with one of my young children on my hip or at my feet. Then, over twenty years ago, I attended an introductory dance class taught "for people who shut the curtains at home, and dance!"

The teacher skillfully taught movement and also encouraged the deep physical awareness of sensations of the body. I felt like I had "come home" to dancing again and joined the dance classes called "Moving from Within." Besides gaining physical skill, I learned to drop more deeply into the sensations of dance and movement. I noticed I was opening more to the spiritual and emotional aspects of dance. I learned to dance consciously, as a meditative and healing process.

We were offered a meditation encouraging us to move out of our thinking minds and drop into the sensations of our bodies, to ground and merge with the elements of nature and the cosmos while dropping into the sensations of what is present to us during our dance. The practice gradually allows the wisdom of the body to guide the dance, and "see what comes up for you".

I often start my dance practice with an idea on how the dance will feel and what will come up for me. My experience reveals when I think my dance will be a certain way, it often turns out to be not what I had expected. When I open up and surrender and allow music to guide the energy of my movement in an embodied, meditative way, there are unexpected opportunities to be with sensation, sound, images, emotions, thoughts in the present moment in new ways.

"It was not what I had expected" truly describes the experience of the dance, sometimes offering a *kensho* moment and sometimes offering an experience that never reaches past the difficulty in physically moving the body. As in sitting practice, one never knows what is going to happen!

The gifts I have experienced from my practice of dancing include a sense of support and grounding, a sense of joy and freedom in allowing the energy and sound of music to "lead" my movements, an invitation to open to the energy of the elements and Earth through the body, as well as a sense of more strength, balance, and a clearer sense of embodiment.

Dance is like life experiences: some good, some neutral, and some judged as "bad." If one is in the present moment, all can be accepted without labeling. What is happening *now* can be held with awareness. Along with personal sense of myself, I discover I am dancing with the Universe.

Dancing from within has helped me deal with a myriad of challenges and internal struggles. One time while dancing, I was feeling a deep sadness about my oldest child, my daughter, leaving home for college. While dancing, I noticed a strong awareness of my lower abdomen, my uterus—my womb—and I was able to feel a grief melded with a sense of love and deep gratitude. A gratitude for having birthed and parented this lovely being. Dancing while cradling my belly was a way to honor my having carried and birthed her. I felt a sense of still holding her with me and also a stronger sense of releasing her to her own life.

Another experience is what I call "being danced." This is a surrender to being so embodied in the music that I feel I am simply the container for these joyous and almost effortless responses to the energy of the dance!

Appendix

How to practice moving from within

Prepare for your dance practice in a space where you can move with comfort either when alone or a safe and supportive group situation. Find music that resonates with you. Perhaps start with slower music, gradually choose music that is medium tempo and rhythmic, then choose selections that have a faster or less predictable tempo. Selecting music as you are practicing can offer natural breaks for sensing what you are needing next. As you near the end of your dance practice, it is helpful to use some movement that invites flow. Then shift to slower movements that can eventually end in stillness.

The key to this practice is to drop into the sensations of the body—just as we do when sitting zazen and practicing mindfulness in ordinary activities. Drop into the present moment with movement and music instead of using a stillness practice. When you have so much energy swirling within the body or so much spinning in the thinking mind, dropping into the sensations and natural movement of the body can be an antidote.

Let movement begin on its own. As you move, experience the gradual opening of body. Be present to whatever kind of movement and sensation comes from the energy of the music. Notice the tendency to be thinking about or planning the dance and allow yourself to open. Simply respond. Let the music inform and guide your movements. Remember not move in ways that do not feel okay or safe for you. Start with small motions and then increase the range or size of you motions as you warm up. Maintaining a stable core and moving in ways that are safe for you, honoring any limitations that you might are initial guidelines. Trust that limitations will change over time. Dance can reveal the unexpected.

A suggestion: Feel the music as it enters your body. Maybe it is begins entering through your fingers or your shoulders, for example. Sense it making a path through and with your body. If the music is entering the through the feet, feel it activating the feet, then legs, through the hips, feeling a sort of spiraling through. For women especially , within the safety of your home, notice how natural it is to move the hips and torso in ways that— out in public—would be interpreted as suggestive but are really just how women's bodies are made to move! The body naturally moves with curves and spirals.

Allow yourself to fully express how your body most naturally moves. Notice the pure joy and sensuality of it all as you safely allow larger the Universal Life energy to move through you. And remember to breathe with the movement, allowing the breath to deepen and support your movements. The breath knows how to nurture and sustain your movements as you relax neck, shoulders, and move from the core. Shaking and putting some spring into your legs is a marvelous way to drop out of the thinking head, and release what every energy and thoughts are not needed, no need to control any of this, the body knows what to do,

Another suggestion: Start with some slower music to ground, warm, and wake up the body. Play some rhythmic music to support the loosening of the hips and torso, then play faster music to support shaking out what is not needed. Even faster music takes one further into the dance, reaching and opening the body from the inside out. Perhaps allow a bit of unpredictability in your movements before gradually discovering a pattern of flow that then allows the body to relax and release into gliding, and graceful expressive movements. Gradually slow down until the body finds rest in stillness. You might stay still in silence or receive an insight or wisdom which emerged from the dance.

As our bodies find and allow deeper expression in response to the music, thoughts and emotions may arise. These can be both from the ego and also from a deeper more Universal wisdom and insight that comes from the opening the small self into the dance.

Just as in any meditative practice this is a gift from the Big Self, from the Source, from Wisdom. It may not may or may not happen but we can be present and trust the unexpected.

Shut the shades! Start the music! Breathe deeply and begin to move. Allow your body to resonate with the vibrations and rhythms of the music. Open up to sensations. Perhaps allow a felt sense of spiraling through, of cleansing, releasing, warming, joyfully engaging your body in movements sensed from within.

Dancing from within holds you both *with* and *in* your body in the present moment. It offers the direct realization of your deep dignity, worth, and beauty. It is an expression of ways the Source of Wisdom can flow through you as a gift to the world.

BIBLIOGRAPHY

Anderson, Reb. *Being Upright: Zen Meditation and the Bodhisattva Precepts*. Berkeley: Rodmell Press, 2001.

Arai, Paula. *Painting Enlightenment: Healing Visions of the Heart Sutra*. Boulder: Shambhala Publications, 2019.

Berry, Thomas. *The Great Work: Our Way into the Future*. New York: Bell Tower, 1999.

The Bible in Today's English. New York: American Bible Society, 1976.

Caplow, Florence and Susan Moon, ed. *The Hidden Lamp: Stories from Twenty-Five Centuries of Women's Awakening*. Boston: Wisdom Publications, 2013.

Chadwick, David, ed. *Zen Is Right Here*. Boston: Shambhala Publications, 2007.

Cleary, Thomas, trans. *The Book of Serenity: One Hundred Zen Dialogues*. Boston: Shambhala Publications, 2005.

Cole-Dai, Phyllis and Ruby R. Wilson, ed. *The Poetry of Presence: An Anthology of Mindfulness Poems*. West Hartford, CT: Greyson Books, 2017.

Conze, Edward C., trans. *The Prajna Paramita Sutra in 8000 Lines*. Bolinas, CA: Four Seasons Foundation, 1973.

Fischer, Norman. Everyday Zen Foundation (online), everydayzen.org/teachings/2018.

Fox, Matt. *Meditations with Meister Eckhart*. Rochester, VT: Bear and Company, 1983.

Gadon, Elinor W. *The Once and Future Goddess: A Symbol for Our Time*. New York: HarperCollins Publishers, 1989.

Ganim, Barbara and Susan Fox. *Visual Journaling: Going Deeper than Words*. Wheaton, IL: Quest Books, 1991.

Gordon, Patricia. *The Epic of Evolution—A Version of The Universe Story.* http//rainforests.org.su/deep-eco/patricia_gordon, 2003.

Hinton, David. *Awakened Cosmos: The Mind of Classical Chinese Poetry.* Boulder: Shambhala Publications, 2019.

Jacobs, Beth. *A Buddhist Journal: Guided Practices for Writers and Meditators.* Berkeley: North Atlantic Books, 2018.

Katagiri, Dainin. Yuko Conniff and Willa Hathaway, ed. *Returning to Silence: Zen Practice in Daily Life.* Boston: Shambhala Publications, 1988.

Katagiri, Dainin. Andrea Martin, ed. *The Light that Shines Through Infinity.* Boulder: Shambhala Publications, 2017.

Kaza, Stephanie, ed. *A Wild Love for the World: Joanna Macy and the Work of Our Time.* Boulder: Shambhala Publications, 2020.

Kim, Hee-Jin. *Dogen on Meditation and Thinking: A Reflection on His View of Zen.* Albany, NY: SUNY Press, 2007.

King, Sallie B. *Buddha Nature.* Albany, NY: SUNY Press, 1991.

Kohn, Michael, trans. *The Shambhala Dictionary of Buddhism and Zen.* Boston: Shambhala Publications, 1991.

Leighton, Taigen Dan and Shohaku Okamura, trans. *The Eihei Koroku, Dogen's Extensive Record.* Boston: Wisdom Publications, 2004.

Loori, John Daido, ed. *The Art of Just Sitting: Essential Writings on the Zen Practice of Shikantaza.* Boston: Wisdom Publications, 2002.

Macy, Joanna and Chris Johnson. *Active Hope: How to Face the Mess We're in without Going Crazy.* Navato, CA: New World Library, 2012.

Manuel, Zenju Eathlyn. *The Way of Tenderness: Awakening Through Race, Sexuality and Gender.* Boston: Wisdom Publications, 2015.

Oliver, Mary. *White Pine: Poems and Prose Poems.* Boston: Beacon Press, 2005.

Purce, Jill. *The Mystic Spiral: Journey of the Soul.* New York: Avon Books, 1974.

Schipflinger, Thomas. *Sophia-Maria: A Holistic Vision of Creation.* trans. James Morgante. York Beach, ME: Samuel Weiser, Inc., 1998.

Suzuki, D.T., trans. and Dwight Goddard, ed. *The Lankavatara Sutra.* Rhinebeck, NY: Monkfish Book Publishing, 2015.

Suzuki, Mitsu. *A White Tea Bowl: 100 Haiku for 100 Years of Life.* Boulder: Shambhala Publications, 2014.

BIBLIOGRAPHY

Suzuki, Shunryu. Trudy Dixon, ed. *Zen Mind, Beginner's Mind: Informal Talks on Zen Meditation.* New York: Weatherhill, 1970.

Tanahashi, Kazukai, ed. *Treasury of the True Dharma: Zen Master Dogen's Shobogenzo.* Boston: Shambhala Publications, 2010.

Uchiyama, Kosho and six others, trans. *Dogen's Genjo Koan: Three Commentaries.* Berkeley: Counterpoint Publishing, 2011.

Wolfer, Jikyo Cheryl, ed. *The Eightfold Path.* Olympia, WA: Temple Ground Press, 2016.

Woodman, Marian. *The Pregnant Virgin: A Process of Psychological Transformation.* Toronto: Inner City Books, 1985.

ABOUT THE AUTHOR

Prajnatara Paula Hirschboeck is the founder and guiding teacher of Sophia Zen Sangha in Madison, Wisconsin. Previously she was Professor of Philosophy at Edgewood College, a liberal arts Dominican school in Madison. There she developed and taught "Philosophies of Earth," "The New Universe Story," "Change Your Mind, Change the World," as well as other courses. She co-founded the college's Environmental Studies Program and a Madison interfaith spirituality center, "Wisdom's Well."

Earlier, during her 25 years as a Dominican Sister, she studied and practiced Soto Zen informally. In the mid-1990s, she began formal Zen Buddhist training with Sojun Diane Martin, founder of Udumbara Zen Center. She was ordained in 2010 and received Dharma transmission in 2016.

Please visit the Sophia Zen Sangha website
for more information:
https://sophiazensangha.org

Photo by Isabel Rafferty, OP

Made in United States
Orlando, FL
20 July 2022

19978614R00112